IGNITION

A PROVEN BLUEPRINT TO CREATE A SIX FIGURE
ONLINE BUSINESS FROM ZERO

BY JAMES FRANCIS

*"I'm at about $10k/month using what you helped me
to develop."*

–Jason Hornung

IGNITION

A PROVEN BLUEPRINT TO CREATE A SIX FIGURE ONLINE BUSINESS FROM ZERO

Ordering Information:

Quantity sales: Special discounts are available on quantity purchases by corporations, associations, and others. For details, contact the publisher at the support desk URL above. Orders by U.S. trade bookstores and wholesalers: Please also contact us at the URL above.

ISBN 978-1-9160836-6-0 Paperback
ISBN 978-1-9160836-0-8 eBook
ISBN 978-1-9160836-1-5 Hardcover

Printed in the United States of America.

First Edition.

DISCLAIMER

Despite the fact I am almost certain you will be much more successful after you finish reading this book and implementing the methods I reveal in it, to be 100% honest and transparent, I legally have to state that no guarantee can be given that everyone who reads this book will gain the same or similar results as myself or my clients. Everything I explain in this book is from my own experience and history. This book is presented for educational and entertainment purposes only and it does not offer any type of professional services advice.

Please do not consider the methods I show you as a "golden ticket" to a better life. Each particular case is unique, every niche has its own positives and negatives, and there are many different factors which make people successful. It goes without saying that in order to reach your goals you will have to take action and actually put in the work. I have put an immense effort in preparing this book for you, but I shall not be liable for any losses you may experience due to the content of this book, as every individual is different, and the content of this book may not be suitable for your situation at a particular moment.

I am considered an expert at what I do, having a huge amount of experience and skills I've acquired over the last 11+ years. Therefore, you should not expect to see any results right away (during the first week, months, or even a year). Your results may be substantially different than what I have experienced, depending on your situation. Ultimately, this depends on many factors, with some of my clients achieving their first $10,000.00 in profit within two weeks and others taking longer than that. So, your results may vary based on many different factors outside of my control.

Please also keep in mind that every third-party service, product or website I mention in this book is my own personal advice only. I cannot make any guarantees as to the quality of or results from these third-party services—you are free to choose whichever works best for you. Nevertheless, I have found those to be the best services and have decided to share them with you.

With that said, everything I teach has worked well for myself and my clients that have followed the steps through to the end, and I hope it will for you too.

ACKNOWLEDGEMENTS

I dedicate this book to all my past, present and future customers and clients, and my team of hard-working employees and freelancers who make this all possible on a daily basis.

Also, to my soulmate, Mischell, who continually gives me inspiration to make our world a better place.

TABLE OF CONTENTS

A NOTE FROM THE AUTHOR

After having my content viewed online by millions of people around the world, I've come to realize that value is often defined by my audience by the results they get from something, and the amount of fun they have while doing it.

So, in this book, you won't find me dancing around a subject for three chapters, talking about my story for what seems like *forever*, while never actually getting to the point unless you buy my more expensive programs. You also won't find me overexplaining concepts just to beef up the word count—I've had to edit enough out already.

Instead, I've written this book to be focused on action, i.e. actually achieving the results you're seeking, even if you don't know what those are yet. I want this book to be the online business results-getting *bible* that is recommended to every beginner online entrepreneur, all around the world. A resource that anyone can use to change their life for the better. A book that every successful online entrepreneur used to get started.

So, you'll be pleased to find worksheets, resources and other free bonuses for each chapter in the online area at www.DigitalProsperity.com/ignitionbonuses, allowing you to apply what you've learned to your own situation and circumstances. Because nothing happens without action.

Also feel free to draw in this book, doodle, read it upside down or whatever helps you achieve your goals.

I also hope to entertain you along the way.

Let's get started...

THE VISION

Open your eyes.

You look at the alarm clock and feel relieved that you don't have to struggle through another early morning.

You hear the sounds of your spouse and kids in the kitchen making breakfast, so you throw on some clothes and go in to join them. They welcome you by jumping on you with a big hug, and you help your spouse with the remainder of breakfast.

You all eat breakfast together. You can't remember the last time this happened, so you cherish how good it feels and how lucky you are to be alive.

"Ok, now hurry up, you'll be late for school!" your spouse says to the kids.

Oh yeah! you think, as you remember it's not a weekend, but actually a normal weekday.

You help your kids to get ready, then join your spouse in the car to take them to school.

As you reach the school, you look around the yard and see stressed out parents everywhere. Late for work. Late for appointments. Late for today's full schedule of activities they'd rather not do. They look at you, wondering how you could afford a nice car when they never see you stressed out or late for work, like them.

You kiss your kids goodbye, then you take a detour to have a spontaneous trip to the beach with your spouse. After all, you have a relaxed schedule and nowhere to be.

You both chat over a cool drink, laughing and joking about old memories and making new ones.

Soon it's time to head home, so you drive back and start your working day.

But this isn't any normal working day, as you can work whenever and wherever you like. So, you grab your laptop, relax in your back yard as you soak up the nice weather and press the "on" button on your laptop.

First you check your emails. Overnight, you received 17 "Notification of payment" emails from your payment processor, in various amounts—including $27.00, $37.00, $97.00, $497.00, and even a few at $3,000.00—and add them to the "sales" folder inside your inbox. You're thankful to receive this money, as every transaction is a sign of *helping* somebody around the world.

Then you sort through and reply to the other emails, ranging from interview requests, to newsletters from people you admire, to questions from your students located around the world.

After spending around 30 minutes doing this, your dog sits next to you for attention, so you playfully rub both sides of his face while baby talking to him. Ok, back to work.

Next, you check your to-do list, categorized into "today," "this week," and "long-term goals."

You focus on the task to write a blog post on a topic you've had a lot of questions about recently, but then after logging in, you realize it's already been written by your assistant. "Nice work!" you tell him via email.

Suddenly you are interrupted with a notification informing you of another "Notification of payment received" email, this time containing another sale for $497. Must have been from yesterday's email newsletter you sent to over 120,000 loyal subscribers.

But you've learned not to procrastinate, so you decide to leave reading the email until later and instead send out the new blog post to your subscribers. You effortlessly write a short email in your own writing style, injecting personality without trying to "sell" anything, and hit send. Ten minutes later, you have 30+ blog comments from people thanking you for your advice and complimenting you for the quality of the products they bought from you.

Now, feeling good about yourself, you check your traffic statistics within your Facebook Ads account. Because you understand the value of tracking and have learned exactly how it works, you can see there are a few campaigns making a huge return on investment (ROI) and some campaigns losing money (i.e. a "negative ROI"). So, you turn off the campaigns that are losing money and scale the winners, knowing this will double your sales over the next few weeks and months.

After doing this maintenance work, you turn off your laptop and decide to spend the afternoon with your spouse eating lunch, sharing moments and doing what you love, before collecting the kids from school later in the day.

When you get home, you chat with the kids about their day and share details about yours. They don't really understand what you do, but they know it makes you happy and helps people around the world. They see that it generates a large income for the family which provides everyone with a great lifestyle, and allows you to live a stress-free life, unlike the soul-destroying job you had before.

This scenario sounds like a pipe dream to most but is a *reality* to those entrepreneurs, like me, who persevere with the correct methods to build a reliable, consistent, mostly-automated online business (except I don't have any kids, yet!).

But I wasn't given this on a silver platter, and I certainly wasn't some overly-exaggerated overnight success story.

It all started when I was fresh out of high school in the United Kingdom and getting ready to attend college. I saw a few ads online to make enough money to get a Lamborghini overnight, and thought to myself, *What could go wrong?* Apparently, a lot can go wrong.

My first website was called "Internet Marketing Profit Machine" (the longest and most scammy-sounding name in history), and I thought it'd be a great idea to have the design as fire coming up out of the page, with money flying everywhere. I only realized after one of my friends was mocking me that I was giving imagery of setting other people's money on fire. Needless to say, I made no money at all. Not a great start!

Then I had to attend college because it was expected of me by my parents and society, and I would be a "failure" if I didn't. I chose to study marketing because I thought it would help me to start and grow my new online venture successfully.

It was supposed to be an exciting and fun time, but the pressure my dad was putting on me to pay the bills and reminding me of the crippling debt made me hate the whole experience. I felt stressed and anxious, but this only made me want to prove him wrong even more.

So, I learned as much as I could about growing an online business and started a new venture as an affiliate marketer—selling other people's products to earn a commission on everything I sold. Back then, it was so much easier, and you could do pretty much anything badly and still make a few sales.

Specifically, I started out my affiliate marketing venture in the "build a chicken coop" niche. I'd never owned any chickens, never lived on a farm and had no desire to, but the little research I'd done told me it was a profitable niche to go into. So naturally I assumed it was a great fit, despite having zero marketing experience, zero knowledge about the niche, and zero life experience at the ripe old age of 18 years old.

After procrastinating for around nine months by gathering as much information as I could without doing anything with it, I decided to finally get myself together. I created a review blog for the products in the niche, did a little search engine optimization (SEO), and started to see traffic in a few days.

After a few months, this one website made me my first few sales online, then my first $100, then my first few hundred dollars.

Instead of scaling it further like I should have done, I went back to the "Internet marketing" niche (the name I knew it as back then, but nowadays I prefer the "online business" niche) and created a new product showing people what I did to make my first few hundred dollars online.

Once it was ready, it was finally time to have a launch for it, so I priced it at $997 on launch day. I sat there in anticipation, watching the clock slowly creep up to my one o'clock launch time. I couldn't wait to be rich and have my own garage of three Lamborghinis!

The clock strikes one, my launch announcement email goes out to everyone I can think of.

Nothing.

I hit refresh a few times, nothing.

Three hours pass, still nothing.

But then suddenly I get an email from PayPal with the subject line as "Notification Of Payment Received." I'd never seen an email like this from PayPal before, so I assumed it was a spam email or some kind of phishing scam, but I opened it anyway. That was the moment my life changed forever.

The email was a notification of $997 being deposited into my PayPal account, online, without me having to go to work or do anything I didn't enjoy. I was ecstatic!

If it's possible to make one sale, it's possible to make more, I thought.

At the time, I had a part-time job at a grocery store (Morrisons, in the UK) stacking bread and cakes on shelves. I'd go to college from 9am–5pm, then work at the grocery store from 6pm until 9pm. I remember feeling like it was soul-destroying, hating every minute I was there, yet putting on a happy face when speaking to people.

But after this eye-opening event of having my first near-$1000 day online, I quit my job the very next day. The feeling of handing in my resignation letter at that job was the best feeling in the world. It was like I was *meant* to do this all my life, and I was finally achieving my destiny.

Soon after, I realized that my college course wasn't really helping me grow my business. So, I quit college altogether to focus on my online business full time.

In hindsight, dropping both my job and college after making just one sale was probably a little premature, but I figured it was finally time to "go big or go home."

And I'm glad I did.

I started learning as much as I could about online businesses while doing freelance work online for other companies, with my little experience. Who knows why they hired me, but they did! All it took was setting up a freelancer profile on UpWork.com, searching for jobs that required the little skills I had, and doing the best I could—and that was enough to fund my business from scratch.

I remember doing all this work from a tiny desk in my girlfriend's (soon to be wife's) parents' house at the time and being forced to pay rent which I didn't have. Every week I'd feel more pressured to pay rent, and every week that fueled me to avoid myself looking like a failure.

Soon enough I had my first $2,000 month. Then my first $3,000 month. Then my first $5,000 month, which is when I bought my first car—a grey BMW 3 Series. At the impressionable age of 20, I felt it was pretty good going to achieve this from my own hard work, and I was pretty pleased with myself.

I was then able to afford to marry my girlfriend. Not just in a normal church, but we actually hired out a whole *castle* for it, with rooms for all the guests and a great party afterwards.

At times, I'd lay in bed thinking over how lucky I was. I couldn't believe that I achieved this from a tiny desk without working for anyone else! It was an incredible feeling.

Since then, I've perfected my craft through thousands of dollars in coaching and over $500,000 in testing, making well over $2.6 million in sales of online products and services (and rising to around $750,000 per year at the time of writing this book), from home, just by helping people to start and grow their online businesses—while working only a few hours a day and living my dream lifestyle.

This is despite not having a clue how to get started, any marketing buddies to rely on, or any kind of start-up capital aside from my $50-per-week job at the grocery store.

To me, being able to help people around the world change their lives for the better is the most important part of what I do, which is why I decided to write this book. I want to give people the same life-changing epiphanies I had, and hopefully I can do the same for you.

So how did I—and do you—get there in the fastest and easiest way possible?

What you're about to read is a culmination of working with over 250+ coaching clients, helping over 200,000+ newsletter subscribers, seeing what works and doesn't work from over $1,000,000 spent on "does X or Y work better?" type tests, and over 11 years of website and marketing optimization.

Or in other words, this book contains everything I would do if I was starting again from complete scratch to get the fastest and best results possible.

It all starts with a dream.

STAGE 1: THE DREAM

Most people begin an online business when life gets tough.

Maybe you're unhappy with your career or day job.

Maybe you feel like you're coasting along in life and the years are passing you by without having achieved your goals in life yet.

Maybe you want to leave a positive impact on the world when you're not around anymore.

Maybe you want your kids, spouse and family to be proud of you.

Maybe you're not living true to your passion or your life's purpose.

Or maybe you just want to live a more financially free lifestyle and not have to worry about money any more.

All these scenarios—and more—often lead to you asking, "How can I make more money?"

At this point, most people do a few web searches, landing on a few "get rich quick" style websites where they tell you about a secret "cash loophole" which provided them with their Lamborghinis, mansions, exotic women and other exaggerated claims. Just pay them $47 per month and you get the exclusive opportunity to promote the same website that pulled *you* in, paying you a commission of every sale you make. How wonderful! You only need to spam your friends and family on social media to do it.

Because of their inflated claims, you see their results as normal and become discouraged when you're not making a 6-figure income three days after starting.

Or, maybe you land on an opportunity to fill in surveys all day for "an endless supply of cash from home." After completing two or three surveys and earning $1.17 for three hours of your time and too many "sorry, you do not qualify for this survey" responses, you get discouraged with that too.

How do I know? Because I fell for both of these "opportunities" myself, not to mention many others when I first got started online.

During this stressful time, my family and friends would often laugh at my plans to make a profit online, and actively discourage me from looking deeper into it because "I should get a real job" like them. I remember my dad actually telling me I was wasting my time and I should work more hours at the grocery store. It's funny how things turn out!

Unfortunately, this scenario of failure and disappointment happens *way* too often at this early stage of your online venture, because you're committing the biggest online business sin— *chasing the cash*, regardless of whether you're actually *interested* in the profit generating activity or not. This isn't a great thing to do, especially if you think back to the reasons you first started looking into this.

With these types of experiences, it's *no wonder* most people think what we do is a scam. I did at first, too!

So how do you move forward from this?

At this point there are two main paths people take:

1) Think everything is a scam and quit, going back to their average life with an average job and a jaded, pessimistic

outlook on every opportunity that passes them by, always wondering, "what if?"

2) They see these initial mistakes as *learning experiences*, regain their optimism, then look deeper into the more *legitimate* business models that aren't promising get-rich-quick type results.

People who take the second path are those who succeed. I know because that's what my many clients and I did to achieve *our* success. The others are still sitting in a forum somewhere moaning about how unfair life is.

I may sound bitter about these "get rich quick" type experiences, but in truth it's these shortcomings that bring you back down to Earth and see this as a real business instead of a "get rich quick" opportunity. You start focusing on a more *real world* approach instead of always looking for the *easier way*.

When you understand that it's truly not possible to get rich overnight and it actually requires you to put in some kind of work, the next question is usually, "How long will this take?", which is a great question.

Personally, it took me around three *years* to reach $10,000 per month online in a near-automated way completely from scratch. Yes, that's a long time. But keep in mind I didn't have a clue what I was doing, didn't bother asking anyone for help, and fell flat on my face more times than a greased up monkey on roller skates.

However, my coaching clients achieved their goals without having to suffer through the same issues, taking them roughly three weeks (yes, that soon!) to around two years, depending on the client.

This vast difference in time frame is based on two things:

1) Your *commitment* to achieving your goals, and…

2) Your existing resources.

First, of course you aren't going to achieve your goals quickly if you see your venture as a hobby that you only invest an hour into every 2-3 weeks.

My clients that saw results quickly were able to invest around 5-6 hours per week (around one hour per weekday, or sometimes a few hours on the weekend), whereas the people that took what seemed like *forever* to achieve their goals seemed to get distracted by their daily life and saw their online success as more of a marathon than a sprint. So, it really depends on how committed you are.

Second, the word "resources" isn't just limited to the amount of money you have to invest, because an online business's growth *isn't* solely based on your budget. Nor is it related to your current authority status or credibility, as that can be created from scratch pretty quickly with the right methods— even if you've never done anything like this before. In fact, we'll talk about how you can generate this authority status from scratch later in this book.

Your resources are a culmination of your current knowledge, problem-solving ability, creativity, determination, amount of time you have to invest, how quickly you grasp and implement new concepts, and more. In other words, how quickly you achieve your goals really comes down to your business IQ and marketing IQ.

An example of a low marketing IQ would be simply stating what you're selling without linking it back to your prospects' need and desires, e.g. "this book has 200 pages and will finally help you to train your dog." Whereas someone with a high marketing IQ understands that their audience doesn't care how many pages a book has, but they *actually* care about the results and life-changing outcomes it can provide them with, in a unique way they haven't heard before—so they focus on this in their marketing.

An example of a low business IQ is making an *emotional* decision to pay for programs, systems and software to sell more effectively when you haven't even decided on your business model yet, meaning many of these will be completely useless to you and an irresponsible use of your available budget. Whereas an example of a high business IQ would be making a *logical* decision to pay $27 per month for a service you definitely need instead of paying the much larger yearly fee upfront, as this decision would free up more capital to be invested immediately in actually acquiring paying customers.

We all start with different business IQs and marketing IQs, but fortunately these can be trained through experience and education.

Once their business IQ, marketing IQ and any other failing elements were improved upon, 100% of my clients (at the time of completing this book, of course) were able to achieve the $10,000 per month online profit when they followed all of the steps I gave them. Yes, that's a 100% success rate. Compare that to a traditional business where 50% of them fail within the first five years *(according to the Small Business Association)*, that's a pretty staggering result.

My goal for this book is to elevate your *online* business IQ and *online* marketing IQ to a level where your decisions are going to give you a boost in profit nine out of ten times. It'll become effortless to you.

But with that said, even if you currently don't have a good marketing IQ and/or business IQ, it's relatively easy to make an online business successful, because it doesn't have as many "moving parts" (i.e. points of failure) as an offline business.

For example, there are no issues with shipping, no issues with inventory, no need to have a huge team of employees, and more.

Now there are three core goals which lead to having a wildly profitable online business:

1) Make a net profit (i.e. you're in positive cash flow with all expenses considered) by selling products and services to people who can benefit from them.

2) Create repeat customers by providing incredible value.

3) Build a loyal audience, preferably in the form of an email newsletter (known as an "email list" in the marketing world).

These are also in order of priority, but they usually all link to each other. For example, it's hard to not make a net profit if you have a lot of repeat customers, and you'll acquire a lot of repeat customers from building a loyal audience and providing incredible value to them.

This means everything you do in your marketing efforts and your business should relate to one of these core goals in one way or another.

… That's it!

Due to there only being three main focuses within the business, average people are starting their new online businesses from home every day. They hear the hype, see the low barrier to entry and want a piece of the action.

But how do you do that, especially if you don't have anything to sell?

STAGE 2: THE BUSINESS MODEL

The digital revolution changed the face of business forever. Never in history has the barrier to entry been *so low* to get started with a profitable business—even more so being able to run it as a one-person team from home.

You don't need a fancy office. The usual cost for this would be thousands of dollars per month, depending on where you live. Instead, you just need a device that can access the Internet and a desk (even *that's* optional!).

You don't need a huge team. Most other businesses are looking at hundreds of thousands of dollars per year for this. Luckily you can do this easily on your own.

You don't need a huge amount of start-up capital. Just a laptop or tablet, a few low-cost website services (e.g. $10 per year for a domain name, $10 per month for website hosting, etc.) and a few low-cost software tools. This is a huge contrast to a 2009 study conducted by the Ewing Marion Kauffman Foundation, where they discovered the average cost of starting a traditional business from scratch is typically over $30,000!

Not only that, but the advancement of the Internet and the "drag and drop" type software tools available mean you don't need to use coding to create websites anymore, so it can be done even if you have *zero* technical experience. If you have enough computer skills to use Microsoft Word, then you have everything you need.

However, all the above only applies to one business model in particular. And it's a business model that has opened the doors to a life of time- and financial-based freedom for me and my students.

Let me explain…

People all over the world are often struggling with one thing or another in their life. But usually it comes under the overall topics of health, wealth or relationships.

Maybe they feel self-conscious and want to lose weight. Or maybe they're happy with their image but just want to look more muscular.

Maybe they're struggling financially and need another way to make extra money. Or maybe they're doing well financially but need a better way to invest and/or safeguard their finances against the future.

Maybe they're in a rough patch of their relationship and they need help. Or maybe they're single and need some dating advice. Or they may even just want to improve their relationship with their dog (i.e. dog training), so it will stop barking at every opportunity.

Whatever you choose, your job is to simply connect valuable products or services (either your own or *other people's*) that solve those issues to people who need them. That's it!

This way, you're able to make a huge positive impact in people's lives at the same time as improving your own life with the profit you generate. Not to mention that when you do this correctly, the traditional way of selling becomes irrelevant, because you'll have people asking YOU to buy your stuff.

I know you probably have a ton of questions at this point, so let's start with the most important part of your business's foundations—which types of products and services you'll be selling.

A lot of people get drawn into online commerce by the seemingly perfect scenario of selling physical products. "No need to create any products or content of my own?! I'm in!" And that's where the cycle of failure usually starts.

If you're trying to sell your own physical products with your own manufacturing and fulfilment process, you have a ton of things to worry about, including:

1) The long development and manufacturing process, where something often goes wrong—not to mention it's so easy to produce too much inventory or not enough.
2) Storage for the products—usually an expensive warehouse or filling your living room to the brim with boxes.
3) Expensive employees to deal with each step of the process.
4) Expensive equipment for each stage of the manufacturing process.
5) Delivery issues, including customers' orders getting lost in transit and you having to send another one (at your cost), with no guarantee this one will reach them on time (or at all!) either.
6) Low profit margins once the product is actually ready.
7) Competition with other sellers selling the exact same thing—meaning you end up competing on price, which is never a good thing when other huge corporations can negotiate lower prices than you.
8) And more!

For a beginner, there are way too many variables (or "moving parts") in this business model for it to be profitable quickly and easily. You can definitely say goodbye to a relaxed lifestyle, that's for sure.

"But what about dropshipping, Amazon FBA[1] or something similar?" I hear you ask!

Sure—this business model does work for a lot of people, but you *still* have some of the same issues as above, including super low profit margins due to the manufacturing and fulfilment process, delivery issues (which always come back to you as the seller, even though you're not responsible), competing with people selling the exact same products as you, and more.

The people who are claiming they've made thousands—or even millions—of dollars after just a few months of starting aren't telling you the full story. They may be making that amount of money, but they usually only take home a tiny percentage of that, typically between 1-5% of their total sales. But of course, those smaller, actual numbers wouldn't help sell their product as well as the bigger numbers, so most of the marketers choose to omit them. This is not too great for all the hassles that come with the business model.

I don't know about you, but personally I'd rather do the work once and collect the profit for life. It's also better to follow an always working, automated, evergreen model than anything else, as too many people burn themselves out with all the work that comes with doing new product launches all the time (such as sucking up to affiliates, constantly creating new products, not having any income between launches and so on), never making the most of their newly-created assets in the *long-term*.

---

[1] Legal note: I do not advertise or disparage this service. It is only a suitable example, which can be changed to any similar service.

That's where digital products and services come in to play.

With a digital product such as a video course, e-book, audio interview series, software or similar, you only need to invest a few weeks into creating them one time, then you're able to sell them over and over again with no manufacturing costs. After all, the product is already created, so delivering the product is as simple as giving somebody a download link, which can easily be done automatically, to be sent instantly after the customer's payment is submitted.

And we haven't even touched on selling *other people's* already-profitable products as an affiliate either, where you *don't* have to create your own products *at all*, so therefore you have zero upfront time requirements or financial costs and earn commissions on every sale you make (sometimes above 75% if you look in the right places).

Less work? Sounds good so far, right? Well the other benefit is the huge profit margin.

With physical products, you're looking at a tiny profit margin of around 10-25% (if you're lucky) after all your other expenses, which makes it tough to surpass your competitors with larger budgets. But with digital products, because there are no manufacturing or fulfilment costs (as everything is done online for free), you keep a lot more of each sale—often upwards of an 80% profit margin after advertising and other minor overheads.

Yep—an 80%+ profit margin.

Case in point from one of my many successful clients:

"Our course sales for June were $41,000...
on about $2,500 in expenses."
–Todd Groskreutz

Because you have more cash to play with, it often allows you to scale your profit a lot faster—with less effort—and gives you a bigger net profit at the end of the year.

That's why I often laugh when I'm watching *Shark Tank*, and the business owner brags how they've made several millions of dollars in sales, yet when it comes down to it, they've only brought home a 5-figure net profit for the whole year.

But this low barrier to entry for online businesses also works against you. According to Forbes, approximately 543,000 new businesses are started every month. That's roughly 18,100 per day!

So, the longer it takes you to decide to get started, the more competitors you'll have and the more difficult it's going to be for you.

That's why I always tell my students to follow the "Ready, Fire, Aim" principle. Just get started and learn as you go along—it's infinitely more profitable that way than waiting until you understand *everything* with 100% clarity. I call this being able to "earn as you learn"—a continuous cycle of implementing new strategies and learning from the results.

STAGE 3: NICHE SELECTION

Now you know how the business model works overall, your first step is to decide on your niche, i.e. what you'd like your online business to be *about*. Here's a simple exercise to decide on this quickly...

Step #1: Write down all the topics you're good at, have expertise in, are passionate about or even just have an *interest* in. Also include your day job if you have one. Don't let the doubts creep in about whether these topics will be profitable or not yet, just write them down.

For example, this could be: Playing the guitar, supercars, watching movies, my day job as a doctor, self-development, mindfulness & meditation, gaming, learning Spanish, focusing on having the best relationship possible with my spouse, travelling the world, interest in marketing, and so on.

I'd encourage you to do this now instead of "later," as "later" rarely happens if you're honest with yourself.

> *Sidenote:* If you find yourself thinking you don't have *any* knowledge, *any* passion projects, or *any* inklings of an interest at all, I'd encourage you to enrich your life with a new hobby which can also be transitioned into a business later down the line.

Step #2: Go down this list and put a star next to the items you already have expertise in. To identify these, ask yourself, "If somebody asked me for help on this topic, would I be able to teach them about it?"

A common mistake is that people think they need to be a *world-class expert* on these topics to make a business out of them. You don't. You just need to know more than the majority of other people in your everyday life do, then they'll *perceive* you to be an expert.

These starred items are important. They are the low-hanging fruit and will typically be easiest to build a business around, because you won't have to learn much about the topic itself.

Or, if you feel you really don't have *any* knowledge on *any* of these topics, put a star next to the items you're most interested in and wouldn't mind *becoming* an expert in by learning about the topic.

But of course, it's not just enough to be knowledgeable about a topic—it should also be profitable, which takes us onto step #3...

Step #3: Now it's time to see which of the items on your list are actually profitable. I call this process "profit validation." Best of all, you can find this out in less than 10 minutes without spending a dime.

First, take the most promising starred item on your list and search for it using your preferred search engine (Google usually works best for me). If one of your passions is something racy then be sure to use incognito mode and check over your shoulder to make sure nobody is watching you. "But it's for work!" doesn't usually cut it.

We're not just looking for generic results here—we're looking for specific profit-producing websites, not just hobby websites. So have a look through the results and try to find websites that are actually selling solutions related to your topic or have some kind of method to earn money from the site ("monetization").

For example, if I search for "mindfulness" and click through to the 10 highest ranked websites, I can see a few of them have a "store" or "products" section. Some of them even have coaching programs at high price points. This type of monetization is a good sign!

At this point, if you recognize the company and/or can see it clearly has a large customer base, you can safely assume it'll be profitable for you too, if you use the right methods.

Sidenote: Don't worry about competing with these people, as the methods we'll be using will minimize any chance of competing with them.

Step #4: Now that we know people are monetizing this topic, we can get an indication of just *how* profitable that monetization is by visiting www.Clickbank.com.

Clickbank is a marketplace for digital products and services, and also provides a way for people to promote these products as an affiliate, earning a commission for every sale you make. As a part of this free affiliate marketplace, it also gives you statistics on how well the products are selling. It's often said, "success leaves clues," and these statistics are a good example of that!

So just click the link in the top navigation bar to visit the affiliate marketplace, and once there, select the topic you're researching in the Categories menu *(the wording of this menu may change over time, but the process remains the same)*.

You'll typically see a list of different products to promote in that topic area, but what we're looking for is at least one product with a "Grav" (short for "Gravity") statistic of 10 or more. This is Clickbank's ranking number for how effectively people are currently selling this specific product.

Note: This doesn't mean a "gravity" of 10 means 10 copies of the product are sold per month, or that 10 people made sales of the product—but it's instead just a general indication of how well a product sells.

Here's an example…

Stats: Initial $/sale: $35.61 | Avg %/sale: 77.0% | Avg Rebill Total: $0.32 | Avg %/rebill: 1.0% |
Grav: 189.28 ←————————
Cat: Health & Fitness : Diets & Weight Loss

Therefore, the higher this gravity number is, the more sales this product makes per month. For example, a product with a gravity statistic of above 300 is probably making a high six figures in sales *per month*, maybe even seven figures. Whereas a product with a gravity of around 10 is probably making around $5,000 per month or less, in total.

The next thing we need to check is, how many products are there in this topic area with a Gravity of above 10?

The more products there are with high gravity numbers, the more profitable this niche is overall.

At this point, you'll be in one of two scenarios:

- **Scenario #1:** Your topic area has at least one product with a Gravity statistic of 10 or more. Congratulations—your topic is profitable!
- **Scenario #2:** Your topic area either can't be found anywhere in the Clickbank marketplace, or it has a

limited number of products with terrible Gravity statistics. Don't be worried if you fall into this scenario, as not all profitable niches have good products on the Clickbank marketplace. The very popular and profitable "business consulting" niche is a good example of this.

Whichever scenario you fall into, we can confirm your topic's profitability and find out exactly what people want by moving onto the final step in this research process...

Step #5: Amazon.com is a marketer's dream due to one simple feature—the reviews section of each product.

Just do a quick search for your topic area in the "books" section of the website, and you'll be presented with a ton of valuable marketing insights. We may not be selling books at all, but this is the easiest method of finding customer feedback in your niche.

First and foremost, if you couldn't find any products related to your topic in the Clickbank marketplace, you should be able to find them here. It won't give you sales statistics, but you can get a rough idea for how well a product sells by the number of reviews. The more reviews a book has, the more total sales it has, and the more profitable your niche is.

Going back to our earlier example of the "business consulting" topic, we couldn't find any products in the Clickbank marketplace, but we can see a ton of books with thousands of reviews on each here on Amazon, so we can deduce that people are buying information on this topic and therefore a business focusing on this topic would be profitable too.

Or in the worst-case scenario, if you're looking at a blank screen because your research doesn't bring up any professional books you can look at reviews for (which you can then apply to your marketing in general), OR the books you find don't have many reviews, it's safer to assume that the niche isn't profitable for *any* kind of products and you should move onto another choice, instead of increasing your risk of failure by "trying it out" for yourself.

In the early stages of a business, it's all about minimizing your risk. And with all the benefits available to you with our online business model, you can do this very easily.

To help you minimize this risk, here's a list of the *most profitable* niches my clients and/or I have made a profit in:

- Fitness
- Weight loss
- Self-improvement
- Mindfulness
- Curing an illness (e.g. diabetes)
- "Internet marketing" / "make money online"
- Business
- Investing (e.g. forex, cryptocurrency)
- Real estate
- Dating & seduction
- Sex / adult (competitive!)
- Marriage advice
- Dog training
- Survival / preparedness
- Music (e.g. how to play an instrument)
- Gambling (e.g. poker)
- Sports (e.g. golf, fantasy football)
- Green energy
- Learning new languages
- Parenting
- Spirituality
- And more!

Of course, this list doesn't contain *all* the possibilities— just the most popular and profitable niches/industries that are *definitely* profitable when you get the correct elements online.

Step #6: After you've chosen your niche, you need to know *exactly* what they want. After all, the more you know your customers in your chosen niche, the better you can serve them and the more profit you'll make.

You should know your prospects like the back of your hand, specifically their:

1) **Demographics**—their *physical* attributes, e.g. age, gender, location, income, and so on.
2) **Psychographics**—their *mental* attributes, e.g. what they think, feel, like, dislike, what frustrates them, what objections they have when presented with a purchase opportunity, the exact words they use when explaining a problem to you (so you can use the same words in your marketing), and so on.

The more you know your prospects, the more your marketing will *connect* with them and the more profitable your business will be.

For example, whenever I'm writing any kind of content or marketing, I often imagine I'm speaking to a 35-65 year old man or woman located in either the UK, Canada or USA, who earns an average wage, probably has kids and a spouse they want to support, who has dabbled here and there in things to make an income online but hasn't really seen it as a proper business until now, is jaded of most claims so will need to see or hear some kind of proof, is hesitant to put in the work until they know it's going to work for them, and so on.

You too should have an "avatar" (a typical representation) of your ideal prospect, otherwise it's going to be difficult for people to connect with what you're saying, as it won't relate to them. As the saying goes, if you market to everyone, you market to no one.

To find their **demographics**, I'd recommend using the Facebook Audience Insights tool. It'll allow you to spy on the demographics of your top competitors' audiences, so you can get a good idea of the demographics for *your own* business, too. Again, success leaves clues!

It's free to use, but you'll need to create a Facebook Ads account first at www.Facebook.com/business/ads . Once signed up, click the Ads Manager menu at the top and click on Audience Insights:

Note: Facebook are always making updates,
so the wording may change.

Once there, select "Everyone on Facebook" from the two options, and type in the names of your competitors in the "Interests" box in the left column, like this:

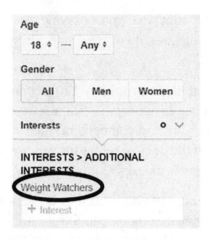

Doing this gives you the demographics you're looking for, like so:

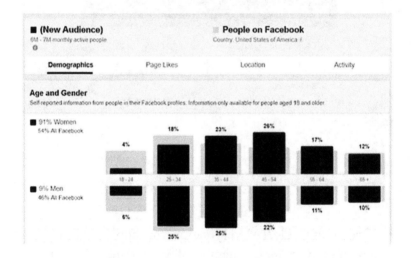

At the top, it shows this specific competitor has six to seven *million* active monthly users on Facebook we can also show ads to. More importantly, it shows us the types of people in that audience. So, from this example, we'd know to tailor our marketing towards women aged between 35-54.

Lower down on the same page, you can also see an assortment of other data, including their typical relationship status, education level, and even the types of jobs they work.

From here, we need to find out your ideal audience's **psychographics**. Thankfully, the Amazon product listings we found in the previous step aren't just for profit validation. They're also for fulfilling the most powerful lesson in business: finding out exactly what your prospects *actually* want, instead of what you *think* they want, or what *you* want to teach. Always keep this at the front of your mind when working on your business—it's important.

Simply read through the positive reviews to see what people liked about a particular product. Specifically...

1) Take the exact phrases they use, including how they say it, and use the exact wording in your marketing.
2) Find out the reasons that drove them to buy the product and incorporate that into your copywriting (i.e. any kind of writing where you're persuading people to do something).
3) See which topics are commonly talked about across all the reviews—these are your niche's hot topics.
4) Read what legitimate issues people are complaining about in the negative reviews and take their advice on board for your own future content and marketing.

In short, use these reviews to get into the minds of your prospects to think as they think, feel as they feel, and sell them a valuable solution that hits their emotional bullseye.

Using the guidance in this chapter, you should have chosen your niche and found out as much as you can about what your prospects are ready to buy, and why. Now it's time to create your website.

But fear not! Fortunately, this is *super simple* with the vast number of technophobe-friendly tools available nowadays.

Here's how to use them to create the best and most profitable website possible...

STAGE 4: WEBSITE CREATION

As you're building an *online* business, it makes sense that you'll need to be *online*. This is even the case if you're selling other people's products, because you'll be acting as a results-increasing *intermediary* between the paid offer and the customer.

Although there are some free website builders out there like Wix.com and similar, these services often place heavy restrictions on what you can do with the website, and you'll often find yourself running into brick walls, having to start again from scratch elsewhere after a week or more of work. It's pretty discouraging!

So instead, I'd recommend setting up your own website. But don't worry! It's actually pretty simple and can be done in less than 10 minutes with the frustration-free tools available to you nowadays.

To get a website online, you need just two things:

1) A domain name, i.e. the web address people see in their browser when checking out your website, e.g. mine is www.DigitalProsperity.com.
2) A hosting account, i.e. the storage for your web pages, files and other stuff which connects to your domain name.

Think of your domain name as your house's address, and the hosting account as the house itself. The two need each other to work properly, as they work together to show your web pages. In other words, when somebody types in your domain name, they are connected to what is stored in your hosting account.

There are tons of providers who allow you to register domain names and hosting accounts for a minimal fee, but my personal favorite for beginners is A2 Hosting. Their servers are faster than most others (including HostGator and GoDaddy, which often cause more problems than they solve, in my experience), their customer support is incredible, and their prices are super low.

You can check them out at the following URL: www.DigitalProsperity.com/recommends/webhosting/. Full disclosure: that's my referral link, so I get credited a few bucks if you purchase through it. Maybe I'll buy a coffee with it or something. If you're against that for some reason, you can simply do a quick web search for "A2 Hosting." But either way, I always recommend this service to all my students and coaching clients because it's the best provider I've found since I started back in 2008.

Once you're there, select a Shared Hosting plan that meets your needs (usually the lowest-priced plan will work for most people, but take a look and see what you think), then simply follow the process they walk you through.

When selecting your domain name, you'll ideally want either:

a) Your first and last name.com, e.g. JamesFrancis.com (that's how I got started). This is known as a "personal brand."

b) A short company name giving people imagery about what you help people to achieve, preferably 2-3 words maximum, e.g. DigitalProsperity.com. This is known as a "company brand."

It really doesn't matter too much, but typically it's good practice to have a company name if you imagine yourself having employees and multiple "faces" to the brand, otherwise operating as a personal brand would be fine.

You'll also want to keep your domain name as short as possible, as there's nothing worse than having to take a gasp for air halfway through reading your domain name out loud because of how long it takes to say. For example, "InternetMarketingProfitMachine.com" (my first ever domain name) was terrible, and "DigitalProsperity.com" was much better because it only has two words and isn't scammy or hypey. Ideally you should try to keep the number of syllables as low as possible if you can, too.

If you're still unsure, look what other experts in your chosen niche are doing. If they're using their own names for their companies, then it's usually a sign that the prospects in your niche respond better to *people* rather than companies, so I'd recommend following in their footsteps.

Just be sure to get the ".com" instead of any others if possible, as the ".com" is still king. There's nothing worse than explaining to people your website is something.co, and they ask you, ".co.uk?" or think it's a typo of ".com" or similar. The ".com" never requires any clarification and is most easily remembered.

If your niche is super competitive and you're struggling to find an available ".com" domain name, then using ".net" is the next best thing—but even then, I'd be tempted to ask other people for some creative ideas to find a different name for a ".com" over settling for a ".net."

If they offer you any kind of upsells or add-ons during the order process for your domain name, feel free to decline them as you most likely won't need them.

Once you've registered your domain name and hosting account, A2 Hosting will connect the two together for you and your website will often be ready to use within a few minutes.

But what do you put on it?

This is where you make another important choice:

Do you want to create and sell your own products to create your own empire (product creator), or simply sell other people's products for a commission (affiliate marketer)?

Being an affiliate marketer is much easier, as you won't have to deal with product fulfilment or create the product itself, *but* it isn't anywhere near as profitable for a few reasons:

1) You're not creating a long-term brand for yourself, you're doing that for the person you're promoting.

2) You're not creating a legacy for yourself, you're just passing people over to someone else for them to get all the recognition.

3) You're not able to edit the sales process or upsell process to match how *you* want to sell the product, which can result in issues making sales.

4) You're not able to edit the product(s) you're promoting, so often the content they teach may not align with your ideals or what you want to teach.

5) Your profit margin will be less than selling your own products, as you're only receiving a percentage of the sale.

6) Sometimes the affiliate program can get shut down, forfeiting all your commissions and leaving you with the task of starting all over again. People promoting the MOBE affiliate program lost tens of thousands of

dollars in commissions after that program got shut down by the feds for bad practices and left a lot of people deep in the hole.

7) Many services such as advertising networks, PayPal and similar are rejecting affiliate marketers due to the high risk they bring with them, mainly due to people using inflated claims, fake stories and other unethical practices. So, you could find yourself getting tarnished with the same brush, and therefore having your accounts banned and payment services holding your money to ransom (like a client who previously had $12,000 of his money held by PayPal for *over a year* before he saw the light and became a product creator).

8) Personally, I feel it's a little "snake oil salesperson-y," as you're passing people to a different "expert" every time you promote a new product, which is often several times per week to maximize your profit. In other words, what you're creating is a series of promotions rather than a long-term, dependable business.

Not only that, but it often involves just as much work—if not more—to get a website online selling other people's products as an affiliate as it does to sell your own products, as you're no longer having to persuade them about yourself, but *also* about another person, too.

Some people may disagree with me and say, "But affiliate marketers X and Y are making a whole bunch of money!" But if you look closer at their business, they'll often have products of their own too.

So overall, solely doing affiliate marketing is a much higher risk strategy to generate a much lower profit.

However, if you're looking for a low-effort "getting used to things" approach and aren't bothered about getting life-changing results any time soon, affiliate marketing is a good place to start and to learn as much as you can.

But if you'd prefer to build your own empire instead of somebody else's, while making a higher profit for your efforts, then creating and selling your own products has never been easier—and I'll prove it to you later in this book.

Whichever path you follow, you'll need to get your website online.

Many years ago, you needed to be some kind of web developer to get even the most basic of websites online. I actually took evening college classes on the days of the week I wasn't working in the grocery store *just* to learn how to create web pages—and even by the end of the course, I still wasn't confident enough in my abilities to create a full-blown website. But nowadays everything has been made point-and-click easy to accommodate the average Joe or Jane.

Specifically, WordPress is the best software to use for the home page of your website. Without getting too technical, WordPress is a framework for normal people to build websites without having to know HTML coding or other programming languages. So, it's ideal for entrepreneurs, and free.

To install it, simply use the login details your hosting company gave you when you signed up with them to log into your website's Control Panel (named "cPanel"), scroll down to visit either "Fantastico," "Site Software" or similar (depending on what's available to you), then follow the step-by-step instructions to install WordPress. If you give this a try and find it confusing, you can always contact your hosting company or a web developer for help. You can even find people on www.Fiverr.com who will do this for you for just $5!

If you were to install this yourself from WordPress.org (not the WordPress.com version as that's totally different with many restrictions), it'd probably take you longer than you'd hoped. But with this one-click installation area within cPanel, you can fill in a few form fields and have it installed within a few minutes.

Out of the box, the website will probably not look how you want it to. However, you can customize this using the many different settings and the thousands of themes—free and paid—available around the web. Simply do a web search for "WordPress themes" (or similar) or browse the official site at https://wordpress.org/themes/.

Web design and coding with HTML is beyond the scope of this book, but there are plenty of guides out there to customize WordPress as a complete beginner, found with a quick web search. For example, if you want to customize your navigation menu, you can search for "customize WordPress navigation menu," and so on.

Another great guide to follow is: https://websitesetup.org/customize-wordpress-101/, along with the many tutorials available for free on YouTube.

Going back to marketing advice, you'll usually need these pages on your website:

1) A "Start Your Own Adventure" Home Page

In direct response marketing, the key to getting people to take action is to focus on the one choice you want them to make and *eliminate* as many other choices as possible.

However, in this case, people have no idea who you are or how you can help them—plus you have no idea about *them* and which stage of the buying process they're currently at.

So, imagine this as a "start your own adventure" type page. When they type in your domain name (www.something.com), they land here and click on what interests them the most, i.e. what they're currently *lacking* to make a buying decision.

We've tested a lot of different variations of this, but here's what works well for us:

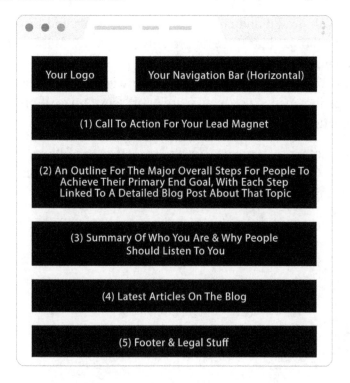

52

Here's why this works so well to both inform new visitors and convert existing visitors…

From top to bottom, we're providing different calls to action (i.e. asking them to do something) depending on their existing connection with you, in order of what we'd like them to do.

Obviously the highest value action we can have them take (with the exception of buying something, which comes later once they know who you are and trust you) is to request something free from you in exchange for joining your email list/newsletter, which is typically some kind of free content like a PDF report or video tutorial. This is known as a "lead magnet," as the valuable content acts as a *magnet* to sign up new leads/subscribers. So, we put that at the top to get as much attention as possible, which is at point (1) in the diagram.

Here's an example:

Logically, if they don't sign up for your lead magnet here, they most likely need more information about how the process you're teaching works, *or* they don't know if your stuff is any good. So that's why we provide valuable advice in separate blog posts in point (2). This way, they can see how valuable your stuff is for themselves.

Here's an example of that on our website:

HERE'S HOW IT WORKS:

Step #1:	Step #2:	Step #3:	Step #4:
CHOOSE A PROFITABLE NICHE RELATED TO YOUR PASSION OR INTEREST	DISCOVER YOUR PROSPECTS' BIGGEST PROBLEMS IN YOUR NICHE	FIND OR CREATE DIGITAL PRODUCTS OR SERVICES WHICH SOLVE THESE PROBLEMS	SELL YOUR SOLUTIONS IN AN AUTHENTIC WAY TO PEOPLE WHO NEED THEM
Learn More About This >	Learn More About This >	Learn More About This >	Learn More About This >

And of course, each button at the bottom of each step goes to a relevant blog post for that topic.

If that *still* doesn't interest them, then they probably want to do their due diligence before learning from you, which is why you give them a short summary about you and a way to learn more about you in point (3) of the diagram.

Here's a visual example of how we lay this out:

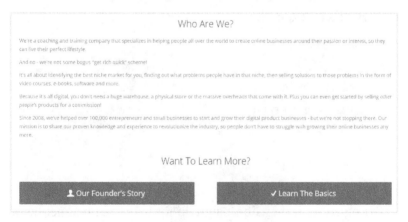

Hopefully the buttons are self-explanatory, but they go to separate pages.

Then after scrolling past all these elements, they'll hopefully have a good idea of what we do, so they can learn about our most recent blog posts—which is positioned at point (4) in the diagram.

Here's an example of that:

Then finally, you should always have a footer section at the bottom of *every* website page, which is point (5) in the diagram. This should include your legal pages such as a disclaimer, privacy policy, and similar—which are available as templates with a quick web search, but I would recommend consulting a lawyer to check everything over just to make sure.

An example would be unreadable when shrunk down to fit on this small book page, but essentially ours has © Copyright Digital Prosperity and the current year, then links to our general disclaimer, earnings disclaimer, terms of use, privacy policy, affiliate disclaimer, comments disclaimer and our support desk.

We've also added links to our social media pages here to get more followers on them, but that's completely optional.

2) An "About" Page

People like to know who they're learning from, so this is mandatory. It should tell people who you are, your story of how you got started in your niche (so your audience can relate) and why they should listen to you.

It should also have a photo of yourself. Some people reading this may recoil in horror about the thought of having of photo of themselves on the Internet, but the truth is, people connect with *people*—not faceless names or anonymous identities. If you don't show the real you, you're going to have a *very* difficult time trying to get people to believe anything you say. This is not 2002 anymore—you need to show people you're a real person if you want them to trust you.

The photo doesn't need to be professional—it can be taken while you're on vacation, in the back yard or anything similar. I'd recommend making sure it's *just* you in the photo, is a flattering photo (or if you have self-confessed "face for radio" like me, as good as you can get), and people can actually see your face to identify you.

If you're using company branding instead of personal branding, you can position yourself as the "CEO & Founder" of your company, then still have all the above elements.

3) A "Products" Page

Yes—this applies regardless of whether you're creating your own products *or* if you're just an affiliate.

After you've created your own products, you should list a summary of each one here, linking to the sales page for each product. Don't do any hard selling here though—just provide a brief summary and let the sales page do the selling.

If you're just an affiliate, do the same thing using the name of "recommended products" instead, following the same principle as above, using your affiliate links for the sales pages of each product.

4) A "Testimonials" Page

This is the page where you can brag about how awesome you are through the voices of your prospects and customers. Simply add as many testimonials as possible about you, your skills or the results you've gotten for people.

This may be difficult when you're just starting out, but the more proof you have of your promised results, the more successful you're going to be.

We'll talk more about testimonials later in this book, but for now, just add whatever you already have. If you don't have any, feel free to forget about this page for now and come back to it later.

5) A "Contact" Page

A website without any way to contact you is a big red flag for the prospect.

"How do I get in touch with you if I buy and then don't receive my access details for the product, or worse, you run off with my money?" is the typical question on every prospect's mind when making a purchase.

Also, some prospects will have one or two simple questions they need answering before purchasing, and as soon as you answer them, you make a sale. But left unanswered, you lose that sale.

So, people need a way to contact you—from both a customer acquisition *and* a customer retention standpoint.

However, if you just write your email address on the page, you're going to get more spam emails than you ever thought possible. At least you'll never run out of Viagra and Rolex watches again (at least I won't, because my inbox is full of those emails)!

Instead, a better way to do this is to install any kind of contact form plugin that has spam protection built into it. This may involve one of those annoying yet effective CAPTCHA puzzles, or a simple "I am not a robot" robot-proof checkbox.

At the time of writing this book, in my opinion, two of the best contact form plugins available for free are WPForms Lite and Ninja Forms, but anything similar is fine if these aren't available for any reason.

Once installed, just a standard name, email and text box for their questions will be fine.

When your business starts getting more inquiries, you may want to upgrade your customer support solution to a fully-featured support desk, like Zendesk or Freshdesk. We personally use Zendesk, but it can get expensive, so this is best left for when you're making above $2,000 in net profit per month.

That's it!

I'd recommend putting links to the pages listed above in the navigation menu at the top of your website, in the same order as I revealed them to you above.

Once you have your website online, it's time to start giving people something to buy.

STAGE 5: VALUE CREATION

Creating your own products can seem daunting at first, because most beginner entrepreneurs think you need to be some kind of expert to create something that people find valuable or have an existing following to sell these products to. However, there are ways to shortcut this process and sell them effortlessly—even if you're a complete beginner and your audience is currently sitting at zero.

Specifically, I'm talking about PLR products. PLR stands for "Private Label Rights," and although there are a few variations of this name, the main premise is that you can buy the rights to other people's products to sell them as your own, as if you created them yourself.

This is completely different from affiliate marketing, where everything you promote is still in somebody else's name. Instead, I'm talking about buying the rights to their products to allow yourself to change the author's name, the content inside it, the branding, the marketing, and everything you can think of to make it your own.

Simply type "PLR store" into your favorite search engine to get a wide selection of results. Some of them will be monthly membership sites, and others will provide a way for you to purchase each product individually.

Just be sure to:

1) Check the quality of the product before purchasing, as some of them are super outdated and look like they were created back in 1999. The more up-to-date it is with the most value being given to the customer, the better.
2) Check the terms of the license associated with the product, as some of them have restrictions on what you

can and can't do. If you really like the product but it has restrictive license terms, you can void the terms if you modify the product by 50% or more, as then it becomes your own property and you can do whatever you want with it. But I'm not a lawyer, so please double-check with a lawyer on this one just to be sure.

3) Usually the best and most valuable products are priced around $50-$100 USD (some priced much higher if they restrict the number of licenses sold), but you can always find bargains below $20 if you look in the right places.

By using this PLR product as a springboard, you can quickly create your own best-selling product line with a fraction of the effort.

That's what I did with a piece of software to create squeeze pages, back in the day when WordPress was very basic and webpage creation tools were difficult to come by. I bought the PLR rights to the software, rebranded it to make it my own, then sold it at $7 with the option to include two products of my own with their order. Doing this, I was able to make a profit on my traffic on day one of people clicking on my ads. It was a good time to be alive!

Just don't fall into the big trap that a lot of other people do and sell them "as is" without any changes—otherwise you'll be doing exactly the same thing as thousands of other marketers and give your prospects no reason whatsoever to buy from you over everyone else. If you do this, the only kind of activity you'll get when you advertise them is a few tumbleweeds blowing from one end of your laptop screen to the other.

However, if you feel you have a lot of value to share with the world and would prefer to do this from scratch, that's great too! We'll talk about the specifics of *how* to do this later.

Whichever path you take, you should always be learning as much as possible while teaching your existing knowledge, even if it's just *one* thing that other people don't know.

For example, when I first got started, I taught people everything I knew about one specific type of web page I'd learned about in my night-time web design college classes. At first, I thought people wouldn't be interested in it, but truthfully people loved it because it helped them to get their message out to the world, and it later turned into the business I have today!

So, don't let any doubts or your lack of knowledge hold you back from your success. Teaching people *anything* that is interesting to them is putting yourself in a position of authority, which results in people instantly seeing you as an authority figure (even if underneath you may be shaking like a leaf). You just need to know one thing about your topic that they don't.

Your audience is then built at the *same time* as this authority status, not before or after.

But if you're not willing to build this authority status as you go along for some reason, you can increase this authority status and credibility pretty quickly in a few ways—even if nobody knows who you are:

1) Learn as much as you can about your topic. The more you know about it, the more of an expert you will be perceived to be.

2) Speak on stage about your topic and get a ton of photos of you doing so. It doesn't need to be a huge venue— even at your local Toastmasters club, networking club or similar would be fine. Whenever you're elevated above other people in a room and teaching them

something, it's always going to make people see you as more of a credible expert.

3) Appear on TV. Any good PR company will be able to get you a slot on a local TV station talking about your topic. Just one short clip of you being interviewed on there will help you to be seen as a credible expert on your topic. We did this for another client in the mindfulness niche and used the video clips in her advertising, and we didn't have a *single* person say, "Why should I listen to you?"—it was magnificent to see.

4) Write a value-giving article and get it published on authoritative websites and media sources in your niche. Again, a PR company could easily help you achieve this. We don't care about the exposure on the actual website here—the most important thing is being able to use an "As Seen On" section on your web pages and in your marketing. For example, getting an article published on Entrepreneur.com would mean you can use "As Seen On" with the Entrepreneur magazine logo. Do this for a whole bunch of popular websites and you'll have yourself a whole selection of logos to use in this "As Seen On" section, which adds a massive amount of instant credibility to everything you say. Here's an example from one of our clients in the niche of saving money on college fees:

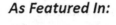

Pretty cool, right? Would you consider that person an expert, even if you didn't know who they were?

Whether you care about the authority status stuff or not, it's not simply enough to *have* a product. You also need to make sure it provides *value* to people, otherwise you're going to get a lot of refunds and very little future purchases of your other products and/or services.

The best way to ensure this is to plan out your product before creating or editing anything, because if you go "full steam ahead!" with the content, you'll often realize you've forgotten to say something earlier on in the product and have to bolt things together like some kind of weird disjointed Frankenstein product.

This planning process doesn't just apply to a single product, either. Ideally your end goal should be to have a *whole suite* of products for different topic areas of your chosen niche. This makes it so much easier to make a profit, while never running out of things to promote.

This *does* sound like a lot of work at first, but remember you only need to do this *once* and you can continue to sell them for several years to come, without much updating or editing at all.

Before you can come up with a plan, you need to identify if you're in a "business to business" (B2B) niche, or "business to customer" (B2C) niche.

A few examples of B2B niches are business consulting, providing services as an agency, social media marketing, the medical arena (e.g. dentists, doctors, chiropractors, etc.), branding agencies, and similar.

Typically, a B2B niche has higher price points and focuses more on services than products, so in this case your plan should include:

1) **An entry-level offer ($497)**—Most people who've never heard of you before are often hesitant to spent $3,000+ right off the bat with you and will need some kind of low-risk transaction to make them feel comfortable with you first. This product or service delivers a good amount of value for the price and gives your clients the results they need to have a natural desire to work with you at the higher price points. My go-to example here is a training program to achieve a specific end goal, delivered in video format—but of course feel free to use your own ideas and creativity here too.

2) **A high-ticket offer ($3,000 - $5,000)**—This is often a group coaching program or 1-on-1 consulting package. I prefer group coaching programs as you're not trading your time for dollars like you would with a 1-on-1 consulting service, plus your results are usually better because there's a motivating sense of community

between your clients. But we'll talk more about this type of offer later in this book.

3) **A super high-ticket offer ($20,000)**—This is often an intensive retreat, a service where you do something for them, or anything with life-changing amounts of value. *Example:* In my business, I build a profitable online business FOR people in a niche of their choice and hand it back to them when it's making $10,000 USD in net profit per month, for six consecutive months. So basically, people trade $20,000 for a minimum of $60,000 back, along with the $10k+ monthly income from their profitable business. The service sold out every time I re-opened it for new clients. High value equals high prices with little resistance, if you're marketing to the right people. Make it a no-brainer for people!

Of course, you can "fill in the gaps" between these price points or have other products or services at the same price points, but this is a good overall flow to start with.

Alternatively, a business to customer (B2C) niche is anything where you're talking to average members of the public, with niches including health, fitness, self-development, mindfulness, survival/preparedness, relationships, dog training, and so on.

They typically have lower price points as your customers aren't "trading dollars for more dollars," so in this case you'll need:

1) **A low-ticket offer ($7-$27)**—Similar to the B2B niche, people will rarely be willing to spend $3,000 in your first interaction, as they need to make sure you can actually help them before they make a large

commitment. That's where this low-ticket offer comes in. Due to the nature of business and the cost of advertising, the sole purpose of this low-ticket product is to break even on any type of advertising spent and acquire a customer into your business, then you make a profit from your other products and services. Some examples include a video course focusing on one aspect of your audience's big goal, a book like this one (yes, this is being used as my front-end offer), an audio interview series, a basic version of a software tool, or anything similar.

This product purchase will also typically be followed by two *optional* upgrades (called "upsells") to maximize the Lifetime Customer Value ("LCV" for short), which will also *complement* the front-end product—not replace it...

2) **An optional upsell ($37)**—In this separate product, you should give them something to swipe and deploy right away to get *immediate gratification*. It's important not to give them another course, as they'll feel they already have enough to go through with your front-end offer and decline it. Also, this product should make sense to people whether they buy your front-end offer or not, as you may wish to swap the order of your products in the future to create a different "way in" to your product line. Some examples include cheat sheets, implementation plans, fill-in-the blank templates, something where you've done some of the work *for* them, or anything similar.

3) **A second optional upsell ($97)**—A more in-depth training around one *more difficult* area of the main

product—or a more advanced topic *not covered* in the main program—usually works best here. For example, a big thing that people struggle with is content creation, so in one of my product lines I offer an upsell where they can legally use other people's content as their own. People can still get some incredible results from using the guidance in the main program but can often *improve* their results and make things so much easier for themselves if they get this optional "content vault" upsell.

4) **A mid-ticket offer ($497)**—As we're stepping up the price point, we also need to step up the value we provide. The best way to do this is provide a service to people, often where you do something *for* them.

In my business, I set up a website, support desk, sales funnel, dedicated customer members area and blog for people—kind of like an online business starter pack.

It's easier to think of an idea for this in some niches than others, but my go-to for niches where this proves difficult is some kind of *personalized* experience.

For example, for one of my clients in the survival/preparedness niche, we created a "survival score" diagnosis for the customer, based on their readiness for an emergency and current skills. After their payment (upfront in full or split between two monthly payments), the customer fills in a questionnaire which is automatically shown to them after their purchase, and my client scores them and sends them ready-made video tutorials to help them improve the areas in which they're failing. Really, this boils down to sending them an assessment of their current situation and giving personalized recommendations to improve.

But any idea would work here as long as you're giving a personalized service of some kind. Primarily this will be sold within your customers' members area and follow-up sequence, but if it makes sense, you can also add this as a third optional upsell to your low-ticket offer to get it some more exposure, with your customers' payment method already in hand.

I've laid out these products in the order that the customer will typically buy them. Some customers will leapfrog some products onto to the next, and some will go straight into the mid-ticket offer from the beginning. But this format is the one that has been the most effective for my business and my clients' businesses.

Notice here that each product does NOT require people to buy the next product in the sequence to actually use their original product. That's the equivalent of selling somebody a car and then telling them they have to pay extra for the wheels. It's a real jerk move, and shady marketers doing this is one of the reasons people become jaded with this industry.

Instead, they should be able to gain a huge amount of value from each product whether they purchase anything else from you or not. The products should be independent of each other, without requiring anything else to make them work. This is not only better ethics, but it'll also increase your customer satisfaction, which in turn will increase your future sales from those same customers – without having to *force* them into buy something grudgingly.

Creating the topics for each offer in your product line is probably the most difficult part to get right, as you need to know exactly what your customers *actually* want, instead of what you *think* they want. These are usually two different things.

For example, people in the weight loss niche will often complain about all the fad diets out there, but then will happily jump right into purchasing a product about one if they see one.

Also, I'd love to create an entire product about having a good business mindset, as it's like trying to swim upstream without one—yet people will happily ignore that and go straight into the "how to" of setting up their business all day long.

So, be sure to spend time revisiting your research around your prospects here, knowing exactly what they want to buy.

If you're still not 100% certain what they would crawl over broken glass to buy, create an MVP. "MVP" stands for Minimum Viable Product, and it means you should create just the *bare foundations of a product* just to get it online, then if people buy it, you can develop it into the full blown product you'd be proud of. You can always refund the customers who do buy at this stage if you feel there isn't enough value in the product to justify the price point you charged them during this test.

I've even known some smart marketers to have nothing inside the download area for the product apart from a note saying something like…

"Thanks for your consideration! This was just a marketing test, so the product you purchased doesn't exist yet. You will be refunded within the next few working hours, and we'll let you know when this product will become available again. We appreciate you helping us serve our audience better!"

… Then also an automated email echoing the same thing, just so they don't miss this message and wonder what's going on. Of course, it goes without saying that you should refund them as promised, too.

This allows you to test different ideas and see which is most compelling to people, *before* putting in any kind of work to actually create the products *until* you know people will actually buy them. Then once you know what people are actually willing to pay for, you can go full steam ahead on creating those products.

If you're doing this, you're essentially testing out your best guesses, so it may take a few different attempts and combinations to find something that works for you. It's essentially like picking a lock—eventually you're going to find a combination that clicks with people.

But if you *do* know what people actually want to buy because you've followed the advice in the research chapter earlier in this book, I'd recommend making a list of the most popular topics people need to know about to achieve their big main goal. From that list, choose the topic that is most requested or talked about as your front-end, lowest-priced offer. This helps you to acquire as many customers as possible so they can pass through your upsell flow.

For your upsells, follow the guidance on the previous pages about what these upsells should include, ensuring the topics make logical sense and don't overlap.

The biggest problem I see with people's upsell flows is that they try selling a product about a topic that the customer assumes is *already included* in the original, front-end product they've just purchased.

For example, if the customer purchases a product which promises to be a "complete system for weight loss," then the first upsell talks about the exercises they need to do to lose weight, this often introduces confusion in the prospect's mind, thinking—*Wait, isn't that already included in the main product?*—and a confused prospect rarely buys.

Instead, try to have your upsells on completely different topics than the front-end offer, yet still related to it. This avoids the "I already have that" objections, which are all too common with most marketers.

You should also ensure the upsell flow makes *logical sense* and follows a *typical pattern of desire*.

An example of a **bad** upsell flow with bad logic would be selling people a package of guided meditations as the front-end offer, then selling them a video course about what meditation is as your first upsell. Logically they *already know* what meditation is by this stage, otherwise they wouldn't have purchased the package of meditations!

Then let's say the next upsell sells them *more* guided meditations, which is also a terrible idea because they haven't had chance to go through the first package yet. Not great!

So how can we improve this?

If they've just bought your front-end product—let's say a package of guided meditations—what would they need to do next? Actually use them! Maybe from your research, you've identified that people struggle with integrating meditation into to their existing busy routine, so they eventually stop meditating and therefore lose the benefits it provides. So, with this in mind, it would make sense to have your first upsell as some kind of "action guide" to effortlessly cement the practice of meditation into their daily routine. This complements the front-end offer perfectly, as the two products work together hand-in-hand.

After they're now able to consistently use the guided meditations due to using the previous upsell, how can they get more benefit from their meditation practice? By practicing *mindfulness* and mindful thinking as a whole in their daily life! So, this would be a great workshop for the second upsell.

Your job as the marketer is to discover what people's problems are, then see if they actually want to fix those problems, and if they do, figure out a way to integrate them into a product line that makes logical sense when ascending from one to the other.

Don't be afraid to spend a day or two on this, starting with 10-15 minutes of research and initial thinking, then coming back to it later. The brain often generates better ideas when you're most relaxed, so don't be surprised if your winning ideas come to you in the shower or when settling down in bed. Just be sure to write your ideas down in your phone or on a notepad for later, as it's easy to forget them when your brain gets sidetracked by something else.

Once you have an outline of the product suite you'll be creating, I'd recommend starting by creating the low-priced product so you can start acquiring customers as soon as possible. Then you can "add on" the upsells as soon as they're finished.

Again, the low-ticket product is not to make a profit. It would be amazing if you could, but due to advertising costs and average conversion statistics, it's pretty difficult to do so. Instead, your profit comes from the "back end"—i.e. your upsells, mid-ticket offers and other offers (explained later in this book), along with any other low-priced products you release or promote in the future.

Typically, most people give up at this stage of building their online business, which is a shame because they haven't even started yet. This is simply because this value creation stage requires the most amount of effort out of all the stages, and you'll feel like the perfect lifestyle scenario in the first chapter is a long way away. But thankfully you only need to do this once!

If you're persistent and determined, you can get all of these products finished within a few weeks. But if you procrastinate, don't find solutions to problems, or don't have much time to invest in creating them, it can take a lot longer. So again, this honestly comes down to how much of an action taker you are.

I've known people to use all kinds of excuses, ranging from "lack of time"—when in reality they watch TV for three hours a day, which could be shortened down to two hours to free up an extra hour every day to work on their business—to not having enough knowledge—when in reality they need to *learn* about their topic to *gain* the knowledge they need—and more. Don't be one of those people, otherwise you'll only continue going around in circles.

If you *are* willing to put in the work your dreams require, then the first thing you need to do when planning out what your products will be *about* is something a lot of people overlook, and they usually end up making little to no sales because of it. That thing is making sure your products stand out in the marketplace in a sea of competitors.

Now this *never* comes down to how much of an expert you are, or even how professional your product is—but instead comes down to a simple formula:

BI + UM + PP + IP = Profit & Freedom

I call this *"The Prosperity Formula,"* and using it allows *any* beginner to have instant authority status, branding and positioning—even if you're just getting started.

It eliminates the "how is your product different?" question from your prospects altogether, because it *creates* a difference, makes it *blindingly obvious* to people and positions your product as the only logical solution for them.

Truthfully, I've had some clients who'd never started a business before use this formula and actually *surpass* their competitors who've been doing this stuff for several years.

The first part of the formula is "BI," which stands for "Big Idea."

If I told you I ran my online business to either:

1) "Make myself rich."

OR...

2) "Make a change in people's lives all over the world with a lifestyle-focused online business, so we can finally live the life we deserve," (which is actually our mission statement, by the way).

... How would each of these impact your view of me? And because of that changed view, would it change your mind about buying from me (or something else from me in the future)? Of course, it would!

Unfortunately, most businesses don't have a "Big Idea," so their prospects *assume* it's the more selfish reason (i.e. "this guy/gal is just after my money"), which reduces their prospects' trust in them—leading to fewer sales.

As soon as you have a more "mission" oriented goal for the greater good, people pay attention because it's completely different to what they usually see AND they want to be a part of it.

This leads to increased sales across the board and more repeat customers.

So, I'd recommend spending around 10-15 minutes thinking of the "mission" of your business, related to the goal you're helping them to achieve. Then use this in your marketing for all your products, with the concept of "sharing your products with the world" being the way for you to achieve that goal.

The second part of the formula is "UM," which stands for your "Unique Methodology."

The truth is, most business owners are stuck in 2009 when trying to sell their solution, as they only talk about the *end result*. For example, "learn how to make money online!" "lose weight now!" or, "learn how to play the guitar!"

But this has been done to death in most niches, so prospects are tired of hearing the same old stuff all the time. It's like how movies that have the same story line as hundreds of other movies don't sell too well—because people are bored of seeing the same stuff!

For example, if I see another movie about teenagers who go to a cabin in the woods somewhere and things don't go to plan, I compare it to the many other movies with the exact same plot line and it completely disinterests me. The sample applies to your products.

So, to stand out from all the other noise, you have to position your solution as being unique in some way—and the most effective way of doing that is by showcasing a unique methodology.

In other words, what is different about HOW the end result is achieved?

How many steps does it take people through? And can you think of a name for those steps, naming it something like...

- The _____ Method
- The _____ Formula
- The 5-Step _____ System
- The _____ Principle
- ... Or anything similar?

If Ryan Levesque didn't put a name to his method, "The Ask Method," he would have stuck to something like "how to ask your customers what they want so you can give it to them," which is infinitely less compelling to people.

See how that works? Create a set process for people to follow, name it, then you instantly have your own unique methodology to stand out from everyone else.

People can't learn your unique methodology by doing a web search for your competitors, because you're the only person teaching it!

This becomes even more powerful if you've actually created an *entirely new* process for people to follow, but it's very difficult to do and isn't really necessary.

So, putting a name to the process you'll be walking people through to achieve the goal you're promising is enough to make people think, "Wow, I haven't heard about this before—maybe that's what I've been missing?!"

Next in the formula is "PP," which stands for *Profit Process.*

If you're wondering how you'll be persuading people who have never met you before to buy something from you, it's made super easy by something called a *"Profit Process."*

(Think of it as an upgraded version of a "sales funnel," if you've heard of that term before.)

We'll be talking about this concept a lot later in this book once you've got something to sell. But for now, just know that it's a series of web pages to eliminate buying objections and ultimately persuade people to purchase your product(s).

The final step in *The Prosperity Formula* is "IP," which stands for "Ideal Prospects."

Trying to target everyone at the same time will only result in you being too broad in your marketing, leading to a lack of sales because everyone feels like it isn't a good enough fit for them.

Instead, you need to choose a segment of that audience which has enough people to support a profitable business.

For example...

- Are you targeting beginners? Or advanced folks?

- Do you want to attract people who are broke? Or people who have money to invest in themselves and their future?

- Will someone with an entitlement mindset (or any other serious mindset issues) be mentally ready to start making massive changes?

Narrowing down on your *ideal* prospects means you'll hit your prospects' emotional bulls-eye because you'll be an exact match for them, removing any doubts in their mind about buying from you.

It also helps you to focus your marketing down onto the exact type of people you want to attract and help, which makes it easier to create content for them.

When all four of these elements are in place and working correctly, we get the fifth and final part of *The Prosperity Formula*... Profit and freedom.

To me, this means making enough money to have vacations whenever you want, spend more time with your family, not have to worry about money any more, and generally feel free of all the stress that the rest of society has to go through.

And creating your own products with this formula in mind is the most effective and easiest way I've found to do that.

Think of this process as the "top down" view for creating your products. It won't take you long, but it will have the biggest impact on your sales after they're created. If your products are *already* compelling to people just by the sheer nature of them, you really don't need to do any hard selling at all.

Next, we need to think of what these products will contain. How do you structure the advice inside them?

It's usually good to use a "sandwich" method when creating "how to" style products:

First, you need to do some positive reinforcement. You should congratulate them on taking action on achieving their goals, and remind them that they've made a great decision because they'll now be able to achieve X, Y, Z. Of course, don't actually say "X, Y, Z," but replace this with the specific goals they want to achieve. This often helps to remove any buyer's remorse after the "adrenaline rush" of buying has passed, and get people excited about actually using your product.

The middle of the sandwich is the content itself. Teach them the process to get to their desired end goals!

After you've walked them through the process to achieve their goals, you complete the sandwich by giving a "top down" recap of what you've just taught them, and what they can do next to move forward.

> *Advanced tip:* It's a good idea to have the "what you can do next" part as a recommendation to join your high-priced, high-value coaching or consulting service to prevent them getting stuck, but this totally depends on whether you want to do that and if you have it ready for people to buy yet. We talk about setting this up towards the end of this book.

Once you have a plan for your products and what they'll contain, here's how to create the main different types of digital content for your products...

1) E-book:

This is an easy one. Simply open up Microsoft Word on PC or Pages on Mac (or Google Docs for free on both operating systems, if you don't have any of these word processors), then start typing. Because it'll be read on people's laptops, tablets and smartphones, you can add diagrams, images, or whatever you like. Throw a photo of a cute cat in there if you like.

I'd recommend getting a cover page graphic created using Fiverr.com, as it'll only cost you below $10 for some sellers and having one will make your product look so much more professional. It really makes a huge difference. Just put this on the first page of your document, and also use it in your marketing when promoting the product.

Just keep in mind that due to the massive number of e-books out there and their limitations at demonstrating things step-by-step (which a video can do better), it's difficult to sell them for above $10 nowadays. But definitely a good option if you want to add a very low-ticket, entry-level $7 product to your arsenal.

2) Audio:

Ever heard a Tony Robbins audio program? Or any kind of audio book? That's the kind of outcome you're going for here.

It's as simple as writing a script, then recording your voice and editing out any mistakes. It's a nice mid-way point between writing your content and being on video.

You'll only need one piece of equipment—a good microphone. Any kind of microphone or headset from your local electronics store that has a "clear voice" / "noise cancelling" feature along with a USB connection will be fine.

I'd recommend not using your laptop's microphone, as it can often pick up a lot of background noise, and apparently customers don't want to hear your kids screaming in the other room when they're trying to listen to you.

But if you want to do this properly and have your microphone last you a while, my favorite microphone for beginners is the Blue Yeti microphone. It has a super professional "podcast" style sound, and it's pretty inexpensive for the great build quality and audio quality you get. You can pick it up from most online stores (such as Amazon) in most parts of the world. I'm not associated with the company in any way—it's just my recommendation from other clients using the same.

Of course, there are many better microphones on the market, but these often come with a much bigger price tag, and when you're getting started, that difference in price would be better spent on acquiring customers.

Your audio can be recorded using Camtasia Studio (both PC and Mac) if you already have it and/or plan to record videos in the future, as this prevents you from having to buy multiple programs and therefore minimizes cost in these early stages of setting up your online business. Alternatively, you can use a specialist audio editing program like Adobe Audition if you don't mind the bigger learning curve to get a more professional outcome.

Be sure to do a few test runs for a few minutes before the actual recording, making sure everything is recording correctly. You wouldn't believe the number of times I've presented something for 30+ minutes, only to realize my audio wasn't set up to record properly, or worse, I had my microphone on mute!

Then it's simply a matter of presenting your material as if you were showing something to a valued friend. After that, you're then free to edit the recording if needed.

Your first attempt may be pretty awkward and frustrating, but it gets easier with practice—to the point where having your voice recorded becomes second nature.

Although audio programs are often seen to contain more value than a written PDF, they still lag behind the perceived value of a video-based training program. Speaking of which…

3) Video:

Video is the king of content—no doubt. And it's only going to become more common.

There are two types of videos you can create, and which one you choose will depend on your confidence.

Your first option is a video focused around *presentation (e.g. PowerPoint) slides.* You never appear on camera, and all the audience sees is you talking them through a series of presentation slides with a voiceover audio track.

This is a great option if you're scared of being on camera, and a way to start feeling comfortable with the video creation process.

To do this, you just need some kind of presentation software like PowerPoint (Windows) or Keynote (Mac), again using Google Slides for free if you don't have access to a semi-recent version of either of those. Then it's just a matter of creating the slides based on what you'd like to say.

Here are a few important tips for this based on 11+ years of recording these types of videos:

1) Make sure you change the slide size/layout to match your screen, otherwise you'll get black borders on either side of your slides, which looks pretty amateur. In recent versions of PowerPoint, the setting to change this is found in the "Design" menu—but feel free to do a quick web search for this if you're unsure.

2) Don't write an entire script for everything you want to say on screen, otherwise people will just read ahead on the screen and get bored of waiting for you to catch up. Instead, just write short bullets to remind yourself of

what to say and speak "off the cuff." This will also sound a lot more natural and friendly, instead of sounding rigid and robotic when reading from a script.

3) Don't have all the bullets show up on screen at the same time, otherwise people will still read ahead. Fix this by using the "animation" option to have each bullet fade onto the screen when you click your mouse cursor or press the right arrow on your keyboard.

4) Be sure to decorate your slides with images that are relevant, as most people need to be entertained while they're learning to remain interested.

5) Show examples and talk about your own experiences to reinforce your points. Don't be afraid to show your personality too, as this is what makes your products yours!

Once your slides are created, it's time to get ready for the voiceover. You'll need a microphone for this, but the same recommendations given previously for the audio format apply here, too. So, revisit that above if you skipped over it.

Ready? You can use something like Camtasia Studio (for both Windows and Mac) to record the slides and your audio at the same time. Just like the audio program, be sure to hit record and do a few test runs for a few minutes, making sure everything is recording properly. Then present your material as if you were showing something to a valued friend. After that, you're then free to edit the recording if needed.

Don't worry if you make any mistakes, as these can easily be edited out of the recording. If I get tongue tied while presenting, I just restart the sentence and edit it afterwards. We all mess up, but the whole process does get easier with more practice.

At first, I would screw up my speaking around 20 times *per minute* of video, as I had zero speaking experience and the thought of presenting anything to anyone terrified me more than having no turkey on Christmas Day. My recordings were often unusable because of all the edits I had to make. But over time, this became less frequent and I was able to show my personality on video instead of just "getting the job done."

I used this method of creating videos for around five years before I built up the confidence to use the second option of recording videos—*real life videos*. They can often be daunting for somebody who isn't used to recording themselves on video, but they always massively boost your credibility, authority status and customer satisfaction, if you have the confidence to try them out.

At first, I would shoot my videos on my smartphone, which worked well for several years. Then after a while, I upgraded to a DSLR camera which I bought *used* from Amazon.com to save money on a new camera—but this wasn't totally necessary, and many great courses have been shot on a smartphone camera.

Just be sure to use a tripod (again, available on Amazon and most other electronic stores) to keep the camera steady, as there's nothing worse than feeling seasick from watching a wobbly camera being held by the spouse of the presenter, occasionally asking, "Is this ok?"

With the tripod, be sure to position yourself in the center of the camera frame, with a small gap between the top of your head and the top of the frame. This is the most basic way of shooting video tutorials, and it looks much better than a portion of your head being chopped off the screen.

Something like this…

Another important thing to consider is your lighting. I used to record my videos facing a window to get as much natural light as possible, as in short, this helps the camera to record the footage in the best quality possible—without any graininess or flickering in the footage due to it trying to compensate for the low levels of light.

You can also have your back to a blank wall, or any kind of clean household background, like your living room, dining room, office, etc. I say "clean," because ideally you don't want any dirty laundry on show, or to give anyone an excuse to email you with, "Clean your house!"

Finally, you'll want to try to minimize any kind of outside noise. This is easier said than done—especially if you live in a busy area. But the less background noise you have, the more professional your videos will feel. So, if you struggle with noise, it may be worth going to a soundproofed video recording studio for a few hours.

Once recorded, your videos can also be edited within Camtasia Studio, or Adobe Premiere if you don't mind the *huge* learning curve for a more professional outcome.

With the correct video quality, lighting, setting and content, your videos *will* look amazing and you'll often surprise yourself at the amount of positive feedback you get.

The biggest mistake I made with my first product was having everything in one video lasting for over two hours. I had a ton of complaints saying they "didn't have time" to go through the content, and a ton of refund requests because they saw me as charging $97 for "one video," and they didn't see the value there.

So, after that, I learned it's often best to split up your content into smaller videos lasting between 10-20 minutes long, rather than one giant video lasting 2-3 hours. People have short attention spans, and often find it overwhelming to go through something that long. But split it up into smaller chunks, and they feel like they're making more progress when they're able to move on to the next video—plus they can easily remember where they left off in the previous sitting.

Something that helps me plan out what each individual video should be *about* (i.e. at which point to split the videos up) is this...

Think about your prospect's journey to their end goal. They'll most likely have "stepping stones" to their big goal. Each stepping stone is a separate video. If the stepping stone is a big topic, split it up into smaller stepping stones so they don't feel overwhelmed. Simple!

4) Software:

Software has a massive perceived value, because prospects feel it removes the element of human error.

However, it does have the highest barrier to entry out of all product formats, because you either need to *be* a programmer or *hire* a programmer.

There are some "design your own software" type software solutions available out there, but these are often very limited and it's usually pretty difficult to achieve what you want with them.

So usually, what most people do is hire a programmer from UpWork.com or similar and get them to create the software for you.

However, this does come at a cost—it's usually the most expensive option out of all of these options, with most *simple* software programs running up development costs of multiple thousands of dollars, and *more complex* software programs costing upwards of 5-6 figures. So, for this reason, I usually prefer creating and delivering my content in the video format.

Once you have your products created in the relevant format, you need a way to deliver them to the customer *automatically* as soon as their payment goes through. This avoids you having to sit at your desk all day, waiting to send orders to people. You could be at the beach, out for lunch or anywhere, and your system is always working for you to give customers what they've paid for.

This also ensures the customer gets a good experience, meaning you get to keep most of the sales you make instead of losing a great portion of them to refunds. I've known launches with bad products and terrible product delivery to have refund rates upwards of 60%, which is ridiculous! But when done correctly, you should keep around 95%-98% of the sales you make, depending on your niche and many other factors.

When I first started doing this, I would simply email the customer a link to a web page with a weird name that people couldn't possibly guess unless they were some kind of genius, like www.DigitalProsperity.com/download1587.html. But then I found out that customers were sharing this page with their friends on social media, so people who didn't pay were getting access to the product for free. Plus, there was nothing stopping people from buying the product to find out the URL where the product was delivered, then refunding and still having access to the product. Not ethical or cool!

Plus, if people had bought multiple products, they were always losing the different URLs for each product.

So instead, I discovered it's best to keep everything together in one dedicated members area. We use a subdomain called "members" for our dedicated members area (making the URL https://members.digitalprosperity.com which looks clean and tidy), but this can be named whatever you like.

Inside it, you should have a navigation menu leading to the following pages:

1) A Welcome / "Home" Page

When people visit your members area, they'll often feel a little lost and overwhelmed with all the possible options. So, this page gives them a general introduction to your dedicated customers' area, where they can find their purchased products (more on this later), and also reinforce their decision to become a customer by restating the benefits they can now achieve with your products. So, for example:

"Now, you're a member of the coolest club on Earth, you'll be able to effortlessly train your dog to obey your every command, meaning no more embarrassments with the neighbors, and a more peaceful home life."

Just adding a paragraph or two like this into our members area reduced the refund rates of our products by a noticeable amount.

Speaking of which, you'll also need...

2) A "Support" Page

When people have questions, they're going to be looking for a way to contact you, so it makes sense to put it in plain sight.

However, you can drastically cut down on the amount of support tickets you have to respond to by anticipating and answering their questions before they even submit a ticket.

This is why we have a Frequently Asked Questions (FAQ) section show up when they click the "Support" link in the navigation menu. We go through the usual questions like, "The videos are stopping and starting, how do I fix this?" "I've lost my login details; how do I get them back?" and so on. We're always expanding this section with the questions we get asked by our customers.

We also use this FAQ section as a way to overcome common objections or common reasons for buyer's remorse, as sometimes the customer will be looking to contact your support desk to ask for a refund. However, if you help them with their problem before they submit a support ticket—refund averted!

As an example, a common reason for a refund in *our* industry is, *"I don't have enough time to implement the steps."* So, we created a tutorial which explains how to build a business from scratch on a busy schedule—essentially around 10 minutes of productivity and time management training—and added a link to it in the FAQ section. Suddenly we started seeing fewer refund requests because of this reason. The total implementation time was around 30 minutes. Not too bad, right?

Not only does adding this FAQ section cut down on the number of support enquiries we receive, but it also often helps the customer *instantly* because they no longer have to wait for a reply to their ticket. So, it's a win/win.

Then of course, we add a link to the actual support page on our main website at the bottom of this FAQ section, which they can visit if their question wasn't answered by the FAQs.

3) A "Products" Section

This is where we actually deliver the product they've purchased.

If it's something people need to download like a PDF report, audio file or similar, you can simply upload it to your hosting account using your cPanel or an FTP program like FileZilla (free)—being sure to upload it somewhere in the "public_html" folder if you have one, otherwise it won't work. I typically create a folder called "downloads" within my "public_html" folder, where I upload all my downloadables.

Once uploaded, simply give a brief introduction to the product and link to the file within your hosting account. If you followed the above recommendation to upload it into a folder called "downloads," the link to the file should be www.yourwebsite.com/downloads/nameofthereport.pdf (as each folder is a forward slash)—obviously replacing your domain name and name of the file.

If you actually try following these steps and find the whole uploading process too technical, you can always find somebody on Fiverr.com to do it for you for a very low price. Sometimes it's better to get things out of the way than spending several days pulling your hair out over something small like this.

For videos, it's often best to upload them to a video hosting service (I prefer Vimeo.com, as their lowest priced plan usually fits most people's needs), then embed the videos in your members area, one video per page. Then you'll be able to create a navigation menu through each page (i.e. video) to make it easy to navigate.

The end goal is to have something like this:

When your products are presented in a dedicated members area like this, the customer feels like they've received more value than just being emailed a .zip file with everything inside—not to mention it's easier for them to follow and prevents overwhelming them.

But what's to stop people sharing this web address and having everyone accessing your paid products for free?

The beauty of WordPress is that you can add plugins, which are simple "add-ons" to enhance the functionality of your website. In this case, we can add a content protection plugin.

There are many of them available, including Wishlist Member, OptimizeMember, S2Member and others, but we've always used ActiveMember360 (ActiveMember360.com) for our clients due to it being easy to use and well-integrated with ActiveCampaign (our recommended email list service). It also comes with a free trial too, which is always good.

This software may not be the lowest priced solution out of the alternatives, but if you consider yourself a complete technophobe, it is usually the easiest solution to set up and use—but it's completely up to you.

Personally, we started with ActiveMember360 then transitioned over to iMember360 when we upgraded our email newsletter service (or "autoresponder") to Infusionsoft, as it integrates better and has way more features—but this is only applicable if you're using Infusionsoft, which will probably only be useful to you if you're making above $5,000 in profit per month.

Using any of these content protection plugins, you can create member profiles and membership levels to be assigned to their profiles. This way, you can have one "level" per product, restrict that product's pages only to people who have the level assigned to their profile, and set up the content restriction plugin to automatically assign the level to their profile immediately after their purchase, so they can access the product right away. Those that don't have the relevant membership level assigned to their profile will be given a page which says something like, "Sorry, you don't have permission to access this page."

So, for example, when I created *The Prosperity Formula*, I did the following:

1) Added the product to the members area.

2) Created a membership level within ActiveMember360 called *"The Prosperity Formula."*

3) For each page of the product within the members area, in the setting that says, "Page Protection", I simply checked the box for *The Prosperity Formula*. This essentially tells the system to only allow people who have the membership level named *"The Prosperity Formula"* to access this page.

I then just set up my customer follow-up sequence within ActiveCampaign to automatically add a tag named *"Customer - The Prosperity Formula"* to the customer's profile when their purchase is successful, and also the same for other products they purchase after that, too. ActiveCampaign then checks for these tags when the customer logs into their account and grants them access to the content depending on which tags they have.

If you'd like a more step-by-step process, this is all covered in the setup tutorials on ActiveMember360's website.

Now if your head is spinning with all the technical stuff, you can get away with *not* setting up any kind of content protection during the early stages of your business, as the likelihood of people sharing your products on a mass scale is pretty slim. However, this is something you'll need to do eventually (especially when you get a larger fan base), so it may be worth hiring someone to set it up for you if you can't seem to figure it out yourself.

So now we have a place for your customers to access their purchased digital product(s), and optionally a way to give access to your customers and lock everyone else out... But how do they actually discover the members area?

Well, the members area should be presented to them at the very end of the upsell process. Although unfortunately, not everyone is going to follow the upsell process through to the end during their order, as some people will just close the window and be left wondering how they access what they've just paid for. That's where your email follow-up sequence comes in.

Your email follow-up sequence is a sequence of automated emails which are sent to somebody one after another, with any delay you specify.

We usually recommend ActiveCampaign to our clients because of their huge number of automation features. Just be sure to slide the contacts slider to the far left on the pricing page and go for the lowest-priced option when starting out, as it can get pretty expensive if you choose the more advanced packages.

In this case, we want the first email to be sent immediately, the second email to be sent the day after they join, and the third email to be sent the day after that, and so on—so one day apart.

In a customer follow-up sequence, there are three goals, achieved in this order:

1) To ensure they have accessed what they've paid for.
2) To reduce refunds.
3) To make more sales of your *other* products.

Note here how the first step isn't just to *give* them access to what they've paid for, but instead to ensure they *have* accessed it.

In 11 years of studying tens of thousands of customers' behavior, we've found that people who never access the product are more likely to refund, because they don't see the value for the money they paid. And of course, once this happens, these people have very little chance of buying something from you again.

But as soon as they actually access the product instead of it gathering digital dust, their likelihood of refunding goes way down—assuming you have a good product designed to actually help them, that is (but this should always be the case).

That's why we have a series of emails (which are added to an "Automation" within ActiveCampaign) which goes out like this:

- **Email #1—Instantly after their order is submitted successfully**—Reinforce their decision to purchase ("Congratulations, you've made a great decision," etc.), give them their login details for the members area, tell them how to access their purchased product(s) within their members area, restate the benefits of how the product will help them now they have access to it, and let them know they can reply to the email if they have any issues.

- **Email #2—The following day**—Check they received their login details yesterday (ask them to reply to the email if they didn't), then explain the different parts of the members area to them.

- **Email #3—2 days after their order**—Share some previous success stories (i.e. testimonials) from other people following/using the product, letting them know that they can achieve similar results if they follow the steps. Give them motivation and inspire them!

- **Email #4—3 days after their order**—Answer the most common objections/complaints you get within the email itself to prevent buyers' remorse, now that their excitement of buying a new product has passed. For example, "How do I make this work if I'm a complete beginner?" "I don't have much time to implement this stuff, what do I do?" "I don't have much money to make this work," and so on. Obviously, some of these examples will be more relevant to you than others, depending on your niche, but the important thing is to anticipate what people's objections are going to be and listen to your customers when they email you with a problem.

- **Email #5—5 days after their order**—Send them some bonus content which leads into another product you want them to buy. In other words, don't just hard sell something else, but instead *help* them with a bonus (i.e. at no extra cost) content that makes them have a desire for that other product or service. Personally, I promote an automated webinar for my coaching program here, as this still delivers value but ends with a recommendation to apply for it—so it's a win/win. Plus, it works better than anything else we've tested. But again, selling higher-priced solutions is covered towards the end of this book.

- **Email #6—6 days after their order**—Promote the same content as yesterday if they didn't click the link, using different copy to reinforce different benefits. You can set up this type of behavior-based marketing with most good autoresponders including ActiveCampaign, Infusionsoft, and I believe Aweber too, and many others.

- **Email #7—7 days after their order**—If you're promoting a webinar, send them another email promoting it, using a "last chance to get it" type marketing angle if possible. Give them a reason to take action now rather than leaving it until "later," which never comes. Or, if you've been sending them some other type of free content (e.g. a video, PDF, or similar), then now you can persuade them to buy the main product in a way that links back to what they purchased originally. In other words, explain the ways in which this new product complements the original product.

It goes without saying that all these emails should be sent from an email address that can actually accept incoming emails, i.e. NOT a "no-reply" type email address.

Using this sequence, our refund rates dropped from around 10% to around 2-3%, and around 5% of our $27 purchasers go on to pay $3,000 to become a coaching client (the industry average for this is about 1-2%). So, it's pretty awesome!

Now you have your products finished and everything is set up to deliver them, you obviously need a way to *sell* them. But how?

STAGE 6: YOUR PROFIT PROCESS

At this point, you should have your front-end (lowest-priced) product ready to sell, along with three upsells, which will be completely optional for the customer.

I know you're probably eager to see some kind of profit and the more excited entrepreneurs may have decided to skip a few things here and there to speed up the process, so let me tell you this…

You *can* launch with fewer upsells or even just your front-end product, but this makes it more difficult to recoup your advertising spend and/or massively reduces any profit you *do* make, i.e. it's like playing a game with two hands tied behind your back.

So, let's assume you've followed the steps and have a front-end offer with three products to be sold as upsells, as any serious entrepreneur should.

After 11 years of trial, error and improvement in my own business and my clients' businesses, totaling multiple millions of dollars in sales, I created a process which has worked to generate a huge ROI (ranging from 2-12X at scale, depending on the niche and offer) in every niche I've tried it in—from selling your products *while* building a loyal audience and generating repeat customers—and I'm going to share the end result with you now.

Your end goal is to have an *automated customer acquisition process* constructed of simple web pages that make sales of your new products and/or services 24/7/365, whether you're at your laptop or not.

The key to achieving this is to *automate everything that can be automated* with web pages and follow-up systems, mimicking personal human interaction as much as possible.

After all, you don't want to be chained to your computer all day long, following up with customers, fulfilling orders and doing things that can be done for you automatically. It's as much about the lifestyle as the profit—and you can achieve both when this process is set up correctly.

The customer acquisition process you'll be building needs to take people from knowing nothing about you whatsoever, to knowing, liking and trusting you enough to make a purchase decision.

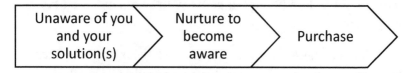

This process is sometimes known as a "sales funnel" (popularized by Russell Brunson), but the process I've come up with, tweaked and improved, is known as a *Profit Process*.

Most people use a sales funnel to build an email list first, *then* make enough sales to break even on their advertising spend within 30 days or less, then make a profit from there.

That's what I did for several years, thinking it was completely normal to be making a huge loss for 30 days after spending money on advertising, only to start seeing a decent profit come in after 2-3 months.

I don't know about you, but I'm not crazy on the idea of being in the hole for a month while I sit there twiddling my thumbs, waiting for people to buy something. So, after a few years of cash flow issues from this now *broken* system, I went about changing that to get a near-instant profit.

That's why when this *Profit Process* is set up correctly, you'll be able to acquire new leads with paid traffic *and* break even on day one, then typically have a 2X return on your investment within 7-14 days, then grow to a 5-10X return on your investment ("ROI") within 6-12 months.

My business typically breaks even within an hour of people clicking our ads and sometimes makes a small profit later in the same day, then makes a 2X ROI within seven days, then makes a 5X ROI within a month, then gradually ascends to a 12X ROI within 6-12 months, depending on where I'm getting my traffic from. Plus, my clients' businesses sometimes get even better results than mine!

So, imagine for every $1 you invest in advertising, you get $12 back. You invest $100, you get $1,200 back. You re-invest $1,000 of that to get $12,000 back. You re-invest $10,000 of that to get $120,000 back... And so on.

An effective *Profit Process* is like having a license to print money on demand. The only thing stopping you from scaling further is the decisions you make about how you want your business and lifestyle to be.

Of course, all of these numbers depend on your niche and many other factors. You could see a lower ROI, or you could see a higher ROI. But either way, you'll find it much easier to make a profit using this process.

Now you're probably thinking you need to be some kind of web designer to create the proven web pages within this *Profit Process*—but you'll be glad to hear that isn't the case anymore.

The introduction of software tools like ClickFunnels, Kartra, OptimizePress and similar has lowered the barrier to entry for the "non-techies" all over the world. Now we can click the screen to edit the page instantly with whatever we want, drag and drop elements where we want them to be, and more. It's like having a connection between your imagination and the web page you're looking at.

Personally, I feel an investment in one of these tools is one of the *best* investments you can make in your online business, as it'll completely eliminate all technical headaches and allow you to create whatever you want to create.

Specifically, I use ClickFunnels for all my clients' projects and for *my own Profit Process* pages, and I recommend the same to everyone. Unfortunately, solutions like OptimizePress don't come anywhere close to it, due to not having order processing capabilities, one-click upsell capabilities, and much more.

You can pick up ClickFunnels with a free trial at www.DigitalProsperity.com/recommends/clickfunnels to see if it's right for you, then it's $97 per month after that (no need for the more expensive options when you're just starting out).

This may sound expensive at first but remember, the end goal is to make a net profit in your business, and this tool is going to make that task so much easier for you—not to mention other order processing services with built-in one-click upsell functionality are priced at upwards of $97 per month alone, *without* any ability to create the other web pages you need to make a profit. So, it's actually a great deal.

And yes, that's my affiliate link and I'll get paid a commission if you visit it and buy through it, however I'd recommend this tool to you whether you use my link or not.

> **BONUS:** As an added incentive, feel free to send me a support ticket at https://support.digitalprosperity.com showing you've bought ClickFunnels through my affiliate link and I'll send you a secret link to import an already-created "fill in the blanks" *Profit Process* into your account, to save you creating it all from scratch. Just spend 30 minutes filling in the blanks and you'll be done. Or if you don't want to buy through my link and get this bonus for some reason, that's cool too.

Either way, once you're inside, it's simply a matter of editing or constructing the pages I'll reveal to you now...

Your *Profit Process* should start with a "sales page." A sales page is a web page with just one focus—to create an irresistible desire within your prospect to buy your front-end (lowest priced) product, so they can achieve their desired result. Think of it like a TV commercial in a web page format.

If you've seen any kind of digital product or service being advertised, you've most likely seen a sales page promising a specific result from buying the product. But try to think of it from a marketer's perspective rather than being on the receiving end as a customer.

As a marketer, the goal of your sales page is to get a high "conversion rate," i.e. the percentage of people who buy a product after viewing the sales page for it. So, if you had 100 visitors to your front-end offer's sales page and three of them bought, that would be a 3% conversion rate for your front-end offer. Similarly, if you had 20 customers view the sales page for your first upsell and 10 of them bought, that would be a 50% conversion rate for the first upsell.

Your goal is to get these conversion rates as high as possible, so you can make more sales and boost your profit. Obviously, a 3% conversion rate is going to make you *three times* the number of sales than a 1% conversion rate from the same amount of traffic, so it's super important to get this right.

And the best way of increasing your conversion rates is making sure your sales message *resonates* with people and aligns with what they *actually* want instead of what you *think* they want.

There are three different ways to present your sales message, to be used in different circumstances:

Sales Page Type #1—The Long-Form Written Sales Letter

This is the type of sales page that seems to scroll down forever. It typically has a large headline at the top, along with a section speaking to the emotions of the prospect, then introducing the product to fix those problems, then providing evidence that the product will help them, and ending with a call-to-action to buy the product.

Nowadays it's best used for products priced below $30, so your prospects can scroll down the page and skim read through the parts that stand out to them, allowing them to make a quick purchase decision.

Here's an example:

Image zoomed out and cropped to show more of the page.

Note the long scroll bar on the right side. Yikes! You may think, "people aren't going to read all that!" but surprisingly some people do when they're reading about something they're interested in, and the others get all they need from skimming through the page and sub-headlines as they scroll down it.

Next up, we have…

Sales Page Type #2—The Video Sales Letter ("VSL")

This type of sales page was first invented by Jon Benson, so full credit to him for that.

With a written sales page, most people will scroll straight to the bottom of it to see the price and make a decision on whether the product is right for them based on the price alone. With products priced above $30, this often leads to people deciding that a product is "too expensive" for something digital—even if they would see it as being worth *a lot more* than that if they'd have actually taken the time to read the rest of the page.

So, the VSL was created to *control the sales process* by showing them a video without any fast-forward controls, which stops people from scrolling down a written sales page straight to the price, and instead shares the value they're going to get from the product to *justify* the price before it's revealed. *Only* when the price is justified and revealed in the video can people click the buy button below the video to visit the order form and make a purchase.

This is important because if they scroll straight down a written sales page to see a price of $497 at the bottom, they're going to think, *Wow, that's expensive!* And close the page without reading any more. But if they are forced to sit through a VSL to first learn the service you're selling is going to save them six months of work and technical headaches and also promises a specific end result or their money back, then that higher price is now justified and is more acceptable to people when it's revealed at the end.

Personally, I feel this is also better for the customer, as this way you can make 100% sure that the customer fully understands what they're buying, instead of people who impulse buy without reading the full page and find out it wasn't what they expected a few minutes later.

For example, we've previously had French people buy our products from a written sales page without them speaking a word of English, then refund a few minutes later for obvious reasons. Go figure!

Using the VSL, I've successfully sold products ranging from $27 to $997 at a huge sales conversion rate and is usually my go-to sales page before testing anything else. So yes, I'll usually create one of these before trying a written sales letter, and only try that if the VSL doesn't convert too well.

The concept of the video is simple. Typically, the message will be presented on slides (created in PowerPoint, Keynote, etc.), with one sentence per slide to keep the viewer's attention due to the fast-changing slides, and the slides read out loud by the presenter as they appear in the video.

Here's an example:

Yep, that's the whole web page. The only thing that changes is the text in the video.

Again, there are no fast-forward controls to prevent people from skipping through the important parts of the message that justify the price.

But where's the buy button?

Only when the price is revealed should the buy button appear below the video. In our case for the above offer, the page then looks like this:

Even then, the page is still pretty short—intentionally. This helps to keep people's focus on the offer being presented to them and nothing else.

As time has progressed and with the rise in popularity of YouTube, prospects have gotten used to better production quality in videos. Case in point, some of you may have thought "Wow, that video looks ghetto!" when seeing the above image, but surprisingly it's not always about how pretty a page looks. In fact, some of the ugliest, most *shameful* pages we've created have made *way* more sales than the beautiful pages we'd rush off to show to our families.

However, this isn't always true, which leads us onto the next type of sales page…

Sales Page Type #3—The Face-To-Camera Sales Video

This is essentially exactly the same as a VSL, but instead of the message being presented in presentation slides, it's presented in-person in a professional face-to-camera video, with images and other graphics added throughout the video for emphasis.

Here's an example:

Because this type of sales page requires more work, I'll usually start by creating a PowerPoint slide based VSL (due to it requiring less production quality, and therefore less effort) and test that first. If it converts well, I'll "upgrade" the video to an in-person sales video like this to see if that boosts results. Usually it does—most likely due to the personal 1-on-1 feel around it and the video being more engaging than following along with words on a screen.

So which type of sales page should you create for your products?

If you're unsure which type of sales page will work best for you, I'd recommend starting with a written sales page, then repurposing it into a VSL, then see which one makes the most sales for you. If the VSL works better, try out an in-person sales video and see if that works better. Then just go with the winner.

Now you have a few options when it comes to writing the words (known as "copy") that go on the sales page…

You can either spend months learning how to write persuasively to get people to buy (known as "copywriting," not to be confused with the legal term "copyright"), or you can hire a professional expert in writing copy (known as a "copywriter") to do this for you.

In the past, I tried writing my own copy, but it became quickly apparent that my sales letter copywriting skills sucked—resulting in low conversion rates—and I found the whole process incredibly boring and difficult. So, after I discovered writing long copy was one of my weaknesses, I started the tradition of always hiring a copywriter to write my sales pages for me.

Yep—the sales pages you may have read on my website weren't always written by me! However, I do always make sure to edit them to match my writing style and "voice," and you should too.

There are plenty of good copywriters out there, and I always recommend one guy in particular to my coaching clients, but if you're not one of my coaching clients, here are two of the best places to look:

1) The "Warriors For Hire" section of WarriorForum.com.

2) Post a job listing on UpWork.com.

However, I always recommend trying the first option before anything else, as you're able to see their testimonials from previous clients.

Specifically, you're looking for copywriters who share results-based testimonials, stating the conversion rates / results they got from their copy. Not just "It was great working with Bob," but specifically, "His copy got a 3.2% conversion rate on my front-end offer," or "His copy allowed me to earn my first six figures in sales," and similar.

If they don't have any results-based testimonials, it's usually a bad sign and I always prefer to find someone else who does. Many of my coaching clients have ended up with lackluster sales page copy by ignoring this advice in the past and losing a bunch of money, so please, don't make the same mistake.

The other thing you should pay attention to is the price they charge. Cheaper is never better. As the saying goes, "Buy cheap, buy twice." In other words, you get what you pay for, and you'll often end up spending more money on a different copywriter after the first one doesn't work out as you hoped.

Although, I once paid a copywriter $10,000 to write copy for one of my products, yet his copy didn't convert at all. So, don't go too wild.

A good price to pay is anywhere between $1,000 to $3,000 to get the sales copy written for your front-end product *and* all your upsells, in total. This may sound expensive, but you only need to pay this fee once, then you can use it for several years to come.

There *are* copywriters who will write a whole sales page for you for below that—but again, the effectiveness of their copy is really hit and miss, so it's always a risk.

Personally, I was hesitant paying $2,000 to a copywriter for my first product (especially as it was a great deal of money for me back then), but that turned into over $200,000 in net profit over the next few years.

The next time I paid a copywriter for a new product, it cost me a little over $3,000, yet that turned into over seven figures in revenue.

That's why I believe hiring a copywriter is one of the biggest ROI-generating activities you can ever do.

When you settle on one, most will send you a questionnaire to complete, asking questions about you, your audience and the product(s) you'll be selling. Usually they'll ask you to send them access to the product, too. After all, they need to know what to write about.

It'll take the copywriter anywhere between 1-5 weeks to finish your copy, depending on their popularity and workload. So, I'd recommend getting the ball rolling on this as soon as you can, to avoid long waiting times where you can't do anything else until you get the finished copy back from them.

Most good copywriters will also help you out if in the rare scenario you test their copy and it doesn't convert as well as you'd hoped. Some will even do a complete rewrite and/or edit it *until* it converts well, so it's always worth asking them instead of struggling in silence. They want to see their copy get good results as much as you do!

Alternatively, if you physically aren't able to hire a copywriter due to lack of funds or similar, then you can always learn how to write long-form sales page copy yourself. A few good resources are *American Writers and Artists Inc* (AWAI), learning from successful copywriting pieces at the swiped.co (note this is ".co" not ".com") website—including the Gary Halbert letters, and any of the expert copywriters including David Ogilvy, Dan Kennedy, Kevin Rogers and more. However, it'll usually take you a couple of months—then sometimes even a few years *after* that to perfect it—so it's worth weighing up the time vs. money sacrifice here.

But whether you decide to write your own copy or get it written for you, there's one thing that will increase your conversion rates—and therefore your profits—overnight: having good testimonials from *other* people saying good things about your product.

It's all well and good *you* saying your product is amazing and will change their life, but why should they take your word for it? It's *much* more convincing if other people are doing the selling *for* you, in the form of them talking about their results in a short testimonial.

Typically, there are three different types of testimonials:

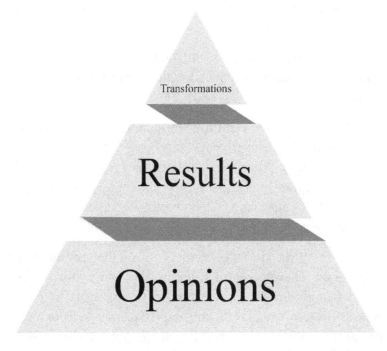

The testimonials from people explaining their "before and after" type transformations are a goldmine. However, they're the most difficult to get, because it requires people to actually do the work (which most people fail to do), put in the effort to create the testimonial about it, and also explain their transformation in an emotional way.

Preferably this testimonial would be in a video format, as these can't really be faked (in a legal way, anyway) and are seen to be more legitimate than written testimonials.

An example of this would be a customer explaining their situation *before* working with you—maybe they were overweight, unhappy to be seen in public, lacking confidence and therefore weren't able to find a partner—*then* their experience working with you meant they were able to lose 30 pounds, which gave them more self-confidence, leading to them finding the love of their life.

It's the negative *before* situation and the life-changing, positive *after* situation which makes this a transformation-based testimonial.

When you get the right transformation-based testimonial, it can literally transform your business overnight. This is because any entrepreneur can *claim* they can help you to achieve something, but as soon as somebody else says you actually did it, your claim is then typically believed with very little resistance.

Lower down in the pyramid are the results-based testimonials. These types of testimonials are usually focused around straight-up facts, i.e. "I used this product to get X result." It doesn't really explain their situation before, and it may not be a life-changing result to them, but it got them *some kind* of positive result.

A few of these results-based testimonials can increase your sales by a significant amount—especially if the results people are speaking about align perfectly with those of the prospect.

For example, if you're claiming your product can stop their dog from barking at the mailman, then you show people a testimonial of one of your prospects explaining how their dog no longer barks at the mailman after using your strategies, then your claim is verified by someone *other* than you, and people will be more likely to believe it, leading to a decision to buy.

At the bottom of the pyramid, we have opinion-based testimonials. These are the most common to receive because it doesn't require your prospects to actually *do* anything with your product, and it takes very little effort for the prospect to write or record them.

An example would be, "At first I was skeptical, but then after going through the product I saw it was what I was looking for and I'd recommend it."

No focus on results, no kind of transformation—just an opinion which in short is saying, "This product is good."

Obviously, if this is in written format, the prospect is going to think, *Anybody can write that!* So, they have little to no power. But of course, if you have no other kind of testimonials, they're better than nothing.

Videos for this type of testimonial are slightly better but are still miles away from the persuasion power that the two other types of testimonials bring to the table.

So how do you use this knowledge to your advantage?

Whenever somebody says something positive about you or your product(s), ask them if they'd be willing to record a short video about it using their smartphone.

Most people will be willing to do this without any issues, but for those who are hesitant, they will often agree if you provide some kind of incentive—maybe free access to one of your other products they haven't purchased yet, an Amazon gift card, or something similar, for their kindness and time spent doing it. Just be sure to disclose this below the testimonial to stay in line with the FTC guidelines.

"Why would you go through so much effort to get good testimonials?" I hear you ask!

Well if you're trying to sell a product without any kind of third-party proof, you're going to find it really difficult to make any sales. Your conversion rate (i.e. the percentage of people viewing the page that actually go through and buy) will be rock bottom, maybe 1% or so.

As soon as you get some really good testimonials, this conversion rate often jumps up to around 5-6%. So, basically, you're increasing your sales by 5-6X just from a few good testimonials. Well worth the effort to acquire the testimonial in the first place.

Obviously, for you to be able to do this, you'll need some kind of existing audience—which you won't have if you're just starting out. This may seem like a catch-22 situation, where you can't get testimonials without having customers go through your product first, but you can't get customers without having testimonials to persuade them to buy. Argh!

A way around this is to join social media groups (such as those on Facebook, which is my preferred channel for this) of people in your niche and offer them free access to the product in exchange for a testimonial. A bonus of doing this is that you can give them guidelines for the format of the testimonial, including the type of topics they should talk about and it being in a short video (no more than two minutes long).

A few things I've learned when doing this with clients:

- I usually give people two weeks to go through the program, implement the steps and come back to me with the testimonial. Although this time period may not be long enough for some people, so you may need to extend it. Really, it depends on how desperate you are to receive them. The lesser the time frame, the more people will stop responding and the less testimonials you'll get.

- Around half of the people who agree to this process will come up with some kind of excuse as to why they can't do it any more—maybe a family emergency, changed priorities, not enough time, and so on. So, I usually like to recruit 20 people to get around 10 testimonials back, knowing only 2-3 of which will be any good.

- Getting people to do something like this for free is like getting blood out of a stone. You'll need to follow up with people multiple times to ensure they're still on track and answer any questions they may have.

It's a lot of work, but it's *so* worth it when you're able to get a 2-3X return on your advertising spend due to your increased sales, because you've gained some proof that your stuff actually works.

Only once you have *at least* 2-3 testimonials (but the more you have, the better), you can consider your sales page finished and ready to use.

After that, you'll probably realize you need somewhere for your prospect to make the payment to you.

Jump for joy—it's time to create an order form page!

We've tested a lot of different order form variations, but there's one layout which usually works best for us across all of the niches we've tried it in. You can see it here:

Of course, the original order form doesn't have the numbers on it—that's just so I can deconstruct it for you now:

(1) The logo is important for branding and also keeping things congruent between the sales page and this order form page, so your prospects feel like they're in the right place.

(2) Instead of a generic title saying, "Your Billing Information" or similar (which typically focuses on loss), we changed this to "Create Your Members Area

Account" (focusing on gain). This increases the perceived value and gives a *purpose* for the information they're giving to you. Notice how we're also requesting the minimum amount of information possible for the order to go through—this increases your page's conversion rate significantly as it avoids the thought of, "I don't have time to fill all those details in now."

(3) By adding a "100% secure checkout" image along with the accepted cards, this helps people to feel their details are safe with you (which they should be). We first give people an option to pay via Apple Pay or Android Pay, depending on the device they're using, as most of our traffic is from people using mobile devices. Not only that, but nowadays Apple Pay and Android Pay are built right into desktop browsers even if they're not using a mobile device. With this option, people can complete their purchase within a few clicks—resulting in our order form's conversion rate increasing by around 10% just from this one method alone.

(4) If they don't have Android Pay or Apple Pay available to them for any reason, they can pay using a normal debit or credit card. Again, we're requesting the minimum amount of information for the order to go through reliably.

(5) It's important to summarize their order before the submit button, just so people feel confident in knowing what they're paying for. Plus, the text "Discounted From $97—Limited Time Only" reinforces the fact that they're getting a good deal while adding a little urgency to submit their order now, rather than waiting and potentially missing out on the discount.

(6) Instead of "Submit Your Order" (yawn), we changed this to relate back to the product they're purchasing. So, it now reads "Access [Product Name] Instantly" (obviously replace this with the name of the product being sold), with the line below it saying, "Get Instant Online Access—Even If It's 2am!" which just reinforces the fact that it's something they don't need to wait to receive.

(7) At the top of the right column, we summarize what they're buying and the *results* it'll give them. This relates the transaction amount back to the results they're going to get, so it's a no brainer for them, i.e. "Wow, only $27 to feel completely de-stressed? I'm in!" You should also have a graphic of the product being sold here, so people have a visual representation of what their money is going towards. If you don't have one created yet, get one, or in the worst case scenario, use a stock photo which matches the end goal your product provides.

(8) People are often hesitant to order from new people or companies—especially when it's online. They usually wonder what happens if they don't like the product and whether they can get their money back without going through a bunch of hassle with their card company or bank. So, it's good practice to remind them of your money-back guarantee here, along with a link to contact you so they can see for themselves you are easily contactable if needed. Alternately, you can test adding testimonials here to see if that works better for you.

(9) Another concern people have is the security of your website and whether their details are going to get intercepted by hackers. So, it's good to remind them of

this here too. *Fun fact: We mistakenly wrote 258-bit encryption here (which doesn't exist—it should say 256-bit encryption) for* three *weeks and over 100 successful orders, and nobody said anything until we noticed ourselves. So, you can still get results even if you screw up!*

(10) It goes without saying that every page on your website should have links to the necessary legal documents like your privacy policy, disclaimer, terms of use and so on, and the footer is the best place to put them. Again, consult a lawyer if you're unsure on which ones you need and what they should say.

Again, all the above can be done within ClickFunnels, and should be there waiting for you if you claimed my bonus for buying through my link.

Using this layout, we're consistently able to get between 40-50% of people who view the order form to complete their order (sometimes more in some niches), whereas the industry standard is around 20-30%. So, I'd say this layout is a good starting point for further testing, or just to use it as is.

After they submit their order, they'll be presented immediately with the first upsell page.

However, you should always start the copy at the top of the page with something like this:

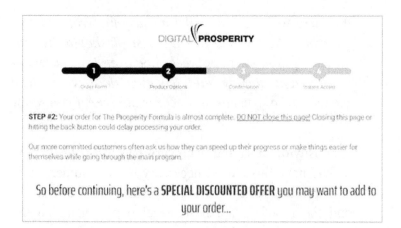

There's one main yet subtle psychological strategy at play here, which makes or breaks the effectiveness of your upsell process...

See where it says, "Your order for [your product name] is almost complete?" The key phrase is *"almost* complete." In fact, this whole section is coming from the angle that the prospect's order isn't finished yet.

We've tested positioning this top section of text coming from the angle of "Your order is complete, congratulations! Would you like to upgrade it?" and every time it's resulted in catastrophically low conversion rates. This is most likely because this angle makes people feel like they can ignore the page, close the window, and generally not pay any attention to this optional process. Whereas, if their order is still unfinished, *they have to pay attention to it to complete their original order*—when realistically their order has already been processed and our system has already queued their welcome email containing their access details to be sent out within 3-5 minutes anyway.

Not only that, but this also lets them know what's going on with their purchase and why they aren't seeing an "order complete" page right now. Without this explanation in place and just showing them another sales page with no context, people always get super confused and call you a scam artist for "stealing their money."

Another important thing to note is the wording of "Our more committed customers..." Everyone wants to feel like they're one of the "action-takers" clan, which leads to people thinking, "hey, this applies to me!"

And finally, upsells work best when they either can't be purchased anywhere else, are discounted from the *original* retail price, or both. So, by adding "special discounted offer," it comes across to the prospect as a customer-only reward, rather than just another opportunity for us to sell something.

The best copywriters say that the "lead-in"—i.e. your first few paragraphs—to your sales page copy will have the biggest impact on your sales, and this particular lead-in copy has worked amazingly well for us across multiple different niches.

Below this, you should just add the normal sales page copy to sell the product, which either your copywriter has written for you or you've written yourself. Just be sure it's positioned from the standpoint of adding this product to their current order, rather than starting a new order.

But above all this, there's one thing that makes a huge difference in your upsell conversion rates—one-click upsell functionality.

Imagine this... Your prospect has just spent about 10 minutes completing your order form with all their details, they hit submit to see the first upsell page, and have to enter all those details in again. It's enough to drive people to close the window and say, "Forget it," leaving them confused about how to access their original order.

So, instead, you can use something called a "one-click upsell" feature. As a non-techie explanation, this essentially stores their order information in their browser *temporarily* while they go through your upsell process, so they can click the "add to my order" button and the page processes the payment using the same details as they wrote on the original order form immediately. This way, they don't need to complete any more forms, their upgrade is billed to their card instantly, and they are then redirected to the next page—which could be your next upsell at this stage, to a maximum of 3.

Most good sales funnel software solutions will have this included, but again ClickFunnels has it included and does an awesome job with it.

Next, it goes without saying that you should also provide a "no thanks" link at the bottom of the page for people to decline the upsell opportunity, which will take them to the next step in the process—again, usually the next upsell at this point, to a maximum of 3.

Two important things here:

First, I say "to a maximum of 3" for both scenarios, because nobody likes sitting through an endless barrage of upsells, and three seems to be the maximum that people will tolerate before becoming frustrated. Of course, some customers are frustrated by one or two upsells, but three seems to be the maximum people are willing to tolerate and is therefore the best option to go with to maximize your Average Order Value (AOV).

Second, you can improve the conversion rate of your upsells by changing the wording of the "no thanks" link to something more creative. Usually, this would involve writing a sentence that people disagree with, so it makes them think twice about clicking it.

For example, for one of my three optional upsells for *The Prosperity Formula*, I offer them a service where we set up a basic website and *Profit Process* for them, priced at $497. Logically, the main reasons why people would decline this upsell are that either they feel it's too expensive, or they can do everything themselves. Realistically, most people are not web designers and therefore with procrastination included, it takes them around 3-4 months to get this technical stuff set up when we can do it for them in 2-3 days. So, we wrote the "no thanks" link as below...

"No thanks James, I'm comfortable implementing all the steps within *The Prosperity Formula* myself. Please take me to the members area on the very next page."

Most people wouldn't say they were "comfortable" implementing all the steps themselves, which leads them to reconsider the offer.

If I had the brass balls to frustrate the *minority* of my customers to result in a greater number of sales in total from the *majority*, I could use something like...

"No thanks James, I'm fairly knowledgeable about the technical stuff like creating web pages, my own content and similar, and I have the marketing skills to make my website compelling to people—without making *any* mistakes or getting stuck—so I'm 100% comfortable implementing all the steps within *The Prosperity Formula* myself. Please take me to the members area on the very next page."

... But personally, I'm not in the business of waving a new problem in somebody's face after they've just spent money with me, as I prefer to nurture my customers in the long-term—not to mention I feel something like this devalues the original product they bought. So, whether you go this far is up to you, but at a bare minimum, you should use a phrase like the one I gave in the first example out of the two above.

So far, you'll have an order process that looks something like this:

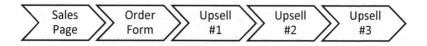

At the end of this upsell process, you'll want to send them to an order confirmation page—preferably within your members area with them already logged into their account, if technically possible with the members area account solution you're using (simply ask their support desk to find out).

I say inside your members area, because you want to put them in a different environment to feel like their order is *actually* complete (which it is, at this point), so they can let their guard down and relax after going through your upsells. This makes them more receptive to what you're about to tell them.

Specifically, here's what the page looks like:

The text may be hard to read in this book, so here's what it says…

> Welcome to The Prosperity Formula!
>
> I'm looking forward to getting you some amazing results and hearing how your online business changed forever, just like the other customers before you who achieved *their* goals.
>
> If you purchased with a credit card or bank account, your statement will show a charge from "JAMESFRANCIS" or "DIGITALPROPSERITY."
>
> You are now logged into your members area account, but your access details have also been emailed to you for your convenience.
>
> (Be sure to check your junk/spam folder in case the emails end up in there by mistake.)

As a **surprise FREE bonus** and as my way of showing you how much I appreciate having you as a new customer, I also want to give you a **free month** of my monthly Digital Prosperity Insiders program.

The price is *usually* $47 per month, which includes 1-on-1 email coaching, premium training from me every two weeks and more—but you're getting **unrestricted access for a full month for 100% free**.

So, click the big button below to learn more about grabbing your free gift, as I can guarantee it'll skyrocket your results instantly...

Click Here Now To Learn More

Once you've claimed your 100% free gift, **click here to access the members area on the very next page and get started**.

See you inside the members area!

- James Francis.
Founder & CEO, Digital Prosperity.

So, we're not only confirming their order details and tying up any loose ends, but we're also making a different, free (i.e. free 30-day trial) offer to them, positioned as a free gift to new customers.

The link to learn more takes them to a separate sales page which explains what they'll get inside the monthly membership program and the terms of the automatic billing after their 30-day trial, so everything is 100% transparent.

Doing this helps your fourth upsell to fly right under the radar, while providing additional value to people who take the free 30-day trial, at no immediate cost to them.

Of course, you should only do this if you have another product to sell—ideally a monthly membership program where you deliver fresh new content to them every month. You don't have to create this right away or before launching, as it's a lot of work to create something like this—but it's good to build up to at some point in the future to boost your monthly profit.

Whether they check out the free 30-day trial or not, they can then click the link to access the members area right away. And that's the end of their order process!

Now, this scenario assumes the prospect is willing to view the sales page, click the button to visit the order form, then place their order without any hesitation.

But not everyone will be ready to view a sales page and buy right away. Some people will need more nurturing than that—not to mention, it's always good to build a loyal audience whenever we can (going back to our three core goals).

So, to nurture those non-buyers to buy, we need to guide them through a value-based process and follow-up with them until they're ready to buy. Some people will take only one or two more interactions with you to make a purchase decision, some people will take more interactions (maybe 6-12), and others will never buy at all. But your nurture sequence is what allows you to do your best to convert the fence-sitters into action-takers.

Typically, around 80% of my sales come from the follow-up sequence, with the other 20% coming from instant purchases. So, if you're getting a 2X ROI from your instant purchases, you'll typically 4X this to an 8X ROI by adding a follow-up sequence.

This is because not everyone will know who you are, trust you or like you enough to buy your product or service right away, and those who don't buy *at all* will often buy a different product from you in future.

I've had people skip my $27 product and other low-priced products entirely, going straight for the $3000 coaching program with no hesitation. But the only way of overcoming those trust-based objections and achieving those future sales is to keep in contact with people until they're ready. The best way to do this is to add them to your email list.

So how do we get these people onto our email list and therefore our follow-up sequence?

Most marketers with a low marketing IQ will simply use a small opt-in form on their blog saying something like, "Join Our Newsletter" or something just as generic. But people's email inboxes are *already* overflowing with emails and spam, and they don't want another marketer flooding their inbox further without good reason. This is why these generic opt-in forms will get a low conversion rate, and it's therefore fairly tough to build a responsive email list this way.

Instead, you can use a combination of valuable free content (called a "lead magnet," named as such because it acquires new leads) and a "squeeze page" to build your loyal audience on your email list.

Here's what our updated *Profit Process* will look like with these extra steps in place:

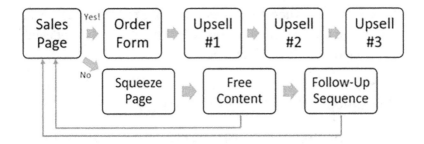

So again, the purpose of both the free content and follow-up sequence is to lead people back to the sales page, this time with an increased desire to buy your product or service. For the smarter marketers out there, the free content is essentially a "down sell" to your primary paid offer if they aren't ready to buy just yet.

But you shouldn't just give this content to people *directly*, otherwise you don't have their details to follow up with them. So, that's why we use a squeeze page…

A "squeeze page" is a simple web page with just *one* focus—to get people to opt-in to your email list/newsletter, so you can follow up with them in future.

When I first started doing this, I thought I was smarter than the average bear, so my squeeze page gave a generic promise like "Discover how to build a successful online business," then after they entered their email address, I sent them straight to my new paid offer I was trying to sell, which gave them the steps to build that successful online business. No free content whatsoever.

Doing this allowed me to follow up with people with an automated sequence of emails, which allowed me to nurture them a little and make my first sales of my own product. But I didn't like the way it felt. It was as if people were entering their email address for a pitch—equivalent to going on vacation and sitting through a time-share meeting, then realizing there was no vacation afterwards. I'm not sure if that has ever happened, but it sounds like it would be terrible.

So, instead, I started to lead with value and focused on helping people. How? By actually helping them!

I created a free PDF report (only about 10 pages or so, including amateur-looking graphics) giving them some valuable advice in exchange for them signing up to my email list, which they found incredibly valuable. This started their thought process of, "Well if his free stuff is great, his paid stuff must be amazing!"

This is the complete opposite of what most people do, where they give away only a small amount of value for free because of the fear they'll have nothing left for their paid products.

But let me tell you this... If they don't like your free stuff, they aren't even going to *reach* your paid stuff! So, it's important to "wow!" them even with your free content. This starts their relationship with you off on the right foot, so they have a natural desire to learn more, instead of you having to force things down their throat by being overly "salesy."

I actually tested this process to find out for sure. I had one version of my website taking them straight to my paid offer (priced at $497), then another version taking them to some free training first. Here are the results:

Variation	Experiment Visits	Conversions	Conversion Rate ↓
● Original - Straight To Sales Video	2,037	4	0.20%
● New Version - Straight To Free Video Training	1,917	6	0.31%

As you probably can't see from the squashed-down screenshot, sending them to some free content first actually made an extra two sales ($994) with 120 less visitors. Not to mention it made me feel better doing it, because I was making a positive impact on people's lives whether they bought or not—instead of feeling like I was putting them under immense pressure to buy.

So, giving the non-buyers a free lead magnet and following up with them about your paid offer afterwards will usually increase your sales in the long term.

But what kind of lead magnet should you create?

The topic covered in your lead magnet will influence the *types of people* you'll be attracting into your *Profit Process*, and if you put trash in, you're going to get trash out.

For example, if your lead magnet is showing people how to get traffic without spending a dime, generally you're going to *repel* the people who *like* spending money on traffic (and therefore investing in themselves and their results), and instead *attract* people who *hate* spending money (and therefore hate spending money on themselves, i.e. your product). So, your sales are going to suffer as a result of this poor marketing hook.

Another example would be having your lead magnet teach strategies for Facebook Ads, then you try selling them something about Google Ads. There's a disconnect there, so you're going to find it incredibly tough to make any sales.

Doing this is equivalent to having a room full of people who raise their hands enthusiastically to learn about dog training, then deciding to teach them about swimming. There's a complete lack of congruence and just doesn't make sense.

Whereas, if the topic of your lead magnet is congruent with the topic of your paid product, then you're going to find it much easier to make sales.

For example, if your paid product teaches them how to use Facebook Ads to get traffic, then it's only logical—and congruent—for your lead magnet to give them a swipe file of 10 of the most effective Facebook Ads of all time. Then your transition from your lead magnet into the pitch becomes easy, as you can say, "Now you know what the best Facebook Ads are, you'll need to know how to set up the campaigns, ad sets and ads in a way that *makes the most* of these types of ads, and also how to *fix* your results if things don't go to plan," and so on.

Another example... Let's say your paid product teaches people how to train their new puppy to be fully house trained. Your lead magnet could teach them just *one* small method from that bigger course, then the marketing hook to buy your full product is easy, as you can say, "This is just one of the 21 other methods we teach in _____," and so on.

In my business, I give people a report for the 12 most profitable niches they can use to build an online business around. By signing up for this report, it's showing me that they're interested in building an online business, otherwise they wouldn't have signed up for it. So therefore, it's an easy transition into the pitch of, "Here's how to make a *profit* in those niches." See how that works?

The purpose of these examples is to show you that congruence between your lead magnet and paid offer comes down to one thing—how easy the transition is between the two?

How easy is it to say, "Now you have X, you'll need to know Y"?

If it's complicated to explain how the two relate to each other **and** there has been no interest shown in the topic of the paid product so far, then you'd be better off choosing a different lead magnet that gives a better connection between the two.

Plus, something that gives immediate gratification usually works better than teaching them something.

For example, in my business, I actually started off with a lead magnet that taught people how to *find* profitable niches online (i.e. do the hard work themselves). After a while, I tested just *giving* them 12 already-researched niches with my findings on each of them, and this version blew the "how-to" style guide out of the water, as they didn't need to do any of the work themselves. Not only were we acquiring leads for half the price of before, but also our sales conversion rate increased *after* they become a subscriber—most likely because they found the latter more valuable.

So really, it's a matter of *giving* people the fish rather than teaching them *how* to fish.

Once you have an idea for what this lead magnet is going to be about, you need to give it a title and a separate marketing hook.

A marketing hook is what differentiates your free lead magnet to your competitors' lead magnets, as it simply states the outcome of your content in a way that sounds compelling to your prospects.

For example, a weak marketing hook would be, "How to train your dog." Every other marketer says that as it requires little to no marketing IQ to come up with, so your prospects are completely *disinterested* as soon as they see it—not to mention they could just do a quick web search for that phrase and see millions of results.

Whereas if you use something like "The 3 Fun Steps To Stop Your Dog From Barking," your prospects don't know what the three steps are, so it makes them more curious to find out and increases the overall desire for your lead magnet.

Better still, you can follow the *Unique Methodology* strategy within *The Prosperity Formula* I gave you earlier in this book to give your strategy a *name,* like "The ___ Method To Stop Your Dog From Barking." This way, your prospects think, *Oh wow, I haven't heard about this before, maybe this will work for me!* Plus, because this name is unique to you, your prospects can't Google it, so they *have* to get it through you. It's instant positioning, authority status and branding, just by the way you word things.

> *Sidenote*: That's why I named my front-end product The Prosperity Formula, as it's infinitely more compelling than "How To Build An Online Business," which anyone can do a quick web search for and see millions of results for. But the name, "The Prosperity Formula," is unique to me. Again, instant positioning, authority status and branding.

You should use this marketing hook whenever you promote the lead magnet—usually as the main headline at the top of your squeeze page.

Now for the title. It should be no more than 7-8 words and a more concise version of your marketing hook, because it shouldn't take forever to say, or have to be written in tiny font just to fit it onto your graphic representing the content (e.g. ebook cover or video thumbnail).

If your marketing hook is already below 7-8 words, you can use your marketing hook as your title. But if it takes forever to say or contains more than 7-8 words, then shorten it down.

For the actual content itself, it should only take you around one or two hours to create it and have it ready to give away, as it only needs to last around 5-10 minutes for a free video and be between 5-20 pages for a free report/PDF.

Regardless of the format, here's what I like to cover in it:

1) **Introduction**—Introduce the problem you're helping them solve and the benefits of solving it. Basically, resell them on why they should pay attention to this.

2) **Who Am I & Why Should You Listen To Me?**—Include a bio photo of yourself and share your story of how you first got interested in the topic, then why they should listen to you (e.g. you've been researching this for a long time, you've achieved the results they're looking for, you have qualifications in this area, etc.)

3) **The Main Content Itself**—Simply teach them what you promised in the marketing hook of the content. Yes, you should actually give them value and don't even mention the paid offer. The most common mistake I see here is people writing 5-20 pages about how the paid product they're promoting will change people's lives, but it shouldn't be about that at all. Instead, actually help people here by giving them something valuable or teaching them something about a topic they need help with.

4) **Recommendation For Your Paid Offer**—This is where you transition from teaching to creating a positive expectation for ("preselling") your paid offer and providing a link for them to check out the full details.

Usually, I'll start this section with a sub-headline that says something like, "So How Do I [Their Big End Goal]?" (for example, "So How Do I Make Six Figures With An Online Business?"), then explain that although the method(s) you've revealed in this free content is important, it's only a smaller part of a bigger system to achieve their big end goal. Be specific with mentioning their end goal, too! Then explain that if they'd like to get the rest of the pieces to the puzzle, they should click the link/button below now. Then of course provide a call-to-action button image—or simply a link if you're not sure how to do that—to your paid offer's sales page.

To wrap all this up professionally, you can also get a cover page graphic created so it looks like a real book on Fiverr.com. Just search on there for "ebook graphic" or similar, then look through the different options available. You can often get one created for just $5, so it doesn't need to break the bank, but doing this will increase the perceived value of the lead magnet, instantly elevating people's opinions of you and your content.

Once that's finished, as a reminder, you shouldn't just link directly to the free content in your ad, otherwise you have no way of following up with them (because they didn't enter their email address to opt in to your list).

So instead, that's why this downsell portion of your *Profit Process* starts by using a squeeze page which advertises your free content, which they need to enter their email address to access, therefore joining your email list in the process. It's kind of like, "Enter your email address to get this free awesome thing in return for joining my email list."

If you're worried about GDPR, doing this is completely fine if you disclose that by entering their email address, they are consenting to signing up to your email list too.

Typically, between 20-40% of people will sign up on a page like this (depending on the niche and how compelling your free content is to people), but here's the page which has gotten the best results for us, that we're still using to this very day:

(Continued on the next page...)

Your Logo

Your Navigation Menu JUST For The Sections On This Page

Visual Representation Of What They Get (E.g. Book Graphic For An Ebook, DVD Case Graphic For A Video, etc)

Big Headline, E.g. "How To____", "6 Steps To ____", "The ____ Method To _____", Etc.

Call To Action ("CTA" For Short) Button To Show Opt-In Form Window

Swipe These [Whatever You're Giving Them] To...

Bullets Containing Features & Benefits, I.e. What The Content Will Do For Them

Call To Action Button #2 To Show Opt-In Form Window

About Your Presenter

Professional (Or Semi-Professional) Photo Of Yourself

Short Summary About Yourself, Your Story And Why You Can Help Them

Some Of The Feedback We've Had From People Using Our Methods

Testimonials From Your Previous Customers

Call To Action Button #3 To Show Opt-In Form Window

Want To Ask Us Something?

Different Style CTA Button To
Your Contact Form / Support Desk

Footer & Legal Stuff

Note: The call to action buttons can say anything you like, but we've had the best success with a mix of "Get Instant Access" and "Download Now."

When they click *any* of the three call to action buttons, the opt-in window appears in the middle of the screen. This contains:

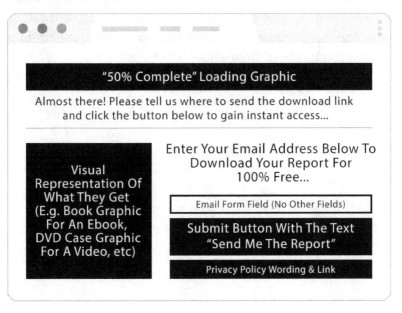

"50% Complete" Loading Graphic

Almost there! Please tell us where to send the download link and click the button below to gain instant access...

Visual Representation Of What They Get (E.g. Book Graphic For An Ebook, DVD Case Graphic For A Video, etc)

Enter Your Email Address Below To Download Your Report For 100% Free...

Email Form Field (No Other Fields)

Submit Button With The Text "Send Me The Report"

Privacy Policy Wording & Link

There are a lot of psychological elements at work on this page and within the opt-in form window, but essentially each section of the page overcomes a specific doubt or question in the prospect's mind as they're reading the page.

It's also important to note that we're just requesting the prospect's email address here, as the more information you ask for, the less subscribers you're going to get. Asking for their name will often take your opt-in rate down a full 10%, meaning you can lose up to 100 subscribers (or more!) for every 1000 visitors you get. So, as the email address is the only piece of information we need to be able to communicate with people, that's all that goes into this form to maximize our results.

When they enter their email address in the form field and click the button to submit it, you can increase your conversion rates in a huge way by giving them what they signed up for right away and then immediately presenting them with a limited-time incentive to buy your front-end product.

Here's an example of what we do...

Thanks! Here's Your Download Link For The 12 Profitable Niches Report...

Click Here To Download It Now

To welcome you to the community, **I've also just activated a "New Subscriber Special"** discount which gives you 72% off our most popular online business-building system, The Prosperity Formula.

BUT - this discount automatically expires when the countdown hits zero, so grab it now below and save yourself $70 before it's too late!

5   23   2   35
DAYS   HOURS   MINUTES   SECONDS

YES! LET ME IN!

100%   VISA

Read on to learn more...

Online Marketing Expert James Francis Finally Breaks The Silence And Reveals The Undeniable Truth...

This Is The Best Time In History To Turn Your Ideas, Hobbies & Passion Into A Profitable, Reliable, Stress-Free Digital Online Business... And I'll Show You How!

Yes, everything below the line that says "Read on to learn more..." is just the normal sales page for the front-end product we tried selling them before.

The limited-time incentive is important here, because we all like to procrastinate, and people usually procrastinate on a *purchase* decision more than anything. If they've said no before, the chances are they need something more enticing to take action—and this is it.

Specifically, I usually give my new subscribers a "new subscriber discount" valid for seven days, starting immediately after they sign up for my free content, taking my front-end product's price down from $97 to $27 during this limited time. This discount should be sizeable and a complete no-brainer to people, not just 10% or 20%. In my example, that's a 72% discount, which helps to get people's attention—even though I intended on selling it for $27 in the first place anyway.

Just be sure to list your front-end product elsewhere on your website for the higher, "normal" price, then you're free to show off the discounted price in your marketing.

Sidenote: I have tested a 72-hour discount and also a 5-day discount, but a 7-day period was the winner—most likely because this time period gives the follow-up sequence enough time to share more value with them and overcome their objections to buying.

The best thing is, because we're promoting the same product as in the other parts of your *Profit Process*, you can simply do either:

a) **Minimum work option:** Give them a coupon code to use on a different order form which states the price as $97, so the coupon code takes the price down to the normal $27 *(minimum work)*.

Or…

b) **A little more work option:** Duplicate the normal sales page, write the price as $97, then cross it out and put $27 next to it with the discount you're giving them, i.e.…

Just ~~$97~~ $27 (72% Off!)

This works even better if you add an evergreen countdown timer next to it, set for a few hours short of seven days, letting them know the discount will expire when the countdown hits zero.

I personally use this option as it works better, and you can see it in action in the previous screenshot.

People love a good discount, and this has always improved our sales conversion rates by a huge margin every time we've tried it, with every client, in every niche. So, it's definitely worth trying for yourself.

This discounted period is also referenced several times in the email follow-up sequence, again set up as an "Automation" within ActiveCampaign if you're using that.

Typically, we like to use something like these with curiosity-based subject lines closely related to the content of the emails:

Email #1:

1) Congratulate them on their decision to get your free lead magnet (but obviously call it a "free video," "free report" or similar).
2) Give them the link to access it in case they missed it (this will be the same page as before, i.e. the one containing the download link at the top and sales page below it with the limited-time discount).
3) Restate the benefits of your product and what results it will get for them.
4) End the email with another link going to the same hybrid download/sales page as before, reminding them of the huge limited-time discount as a new subscriber.

1 Day Delay

(Continued on the next page…)

Email #2:

1) Remind them to *actually* go through your free lead magnet (but again, obviously call it a "free video," "free report" or similar), instead of doing it "later," which never happens. This is important, because we've found that people who have actually gone through your content are much more likely to make a purchase, as they can see the value you provide and often know, like and trust you by the end of it.

2) Give them the link to access your free content again in case they missed it (this will be the same sales page as before, i.e. the one containing the download link at the top and sales page below it with the limited-time discount).

3) Focus on one major benefit of your product, writing in a way to give them mental visions of them living their life after having achieved their goal (called "future pacing")—just like I did at the beginning of this book.

4) End the email with another link going to the same hybrid download/sales page as before, again reminding them of the limited-time discount as a new subscriber.

1 Day Delay

Email #3:

Talk about the life-changing **benefits** (physical *and* emotional) your front-end product will provide to people in a conversational writing style, as if you were writing to a valued friend. Ensure the email contains 2-3 links to the sales page where they can get the full details of the product and how to get started with it (i.e. visit the order form and purchase). Also remember to use the limited-time discount as an incentive for them to take action now rather than later.

1 Day Delay

(Continued on the next page…)

Email #4:

You have a few options here, depending on the marketing resources you have available to you. In order of effectiveness:

1) Show people **your best testimonial or case study**, where your customer is telling the story of how they overcame their issues and achieved their wildest dreams by using the product you're promoting. Below the video, have a button graphic or link taking people back to the sales page.

2) If you don't have a good results-based testimonial, show them some other kind of **undeniable proof** that your system works, such as a scientific study on the *method* taught/used within your product, an appearance in the media, or similar.

3) If you can't find *any* proof of the method you're teaching or the above doesn't apply to you for some reason, tell them **your story** of how you struggled when you got started and then achieved the end result your product is promising.

With all of these options, remind them of the limited-time discount and use it as an incentive for them to take action now rather than later.

1 Day Delay

Email #5:

Again, you have a few options here, depending on the marketing resources you have available to you. In order of effectiveness:

1) Show people **your *second* best testimonial or case study**, where your customer is telling the story of how they overcame their issues and achieved their wildest dreams by using the product you're promoting. Below the video, have a button graphic or link taking people back to the sales page.

2) If you don't have a good results-based testimonial, show them **some *other* kind of undeniable proof** that your system works, such as a scientific study on the *method* taught/used within your product, an appearance in the media, or similar.

3) Again, if you can't find *any* proof of the method you're teaching or the above doesn't apply to you for some reason, this time talk about ***another* major benefit of your product** OR give them **answers to frequently asked questions** directly within the email itself.

With all of these options, remind them of the limited-time discount and use it as an incentive for them to take action now rather than later.

1 Day Delay

Email #6:

Talk about the **logical reasons** why they should grab your front-end product, in a conversational writing style, as if you were writing to a valued friend. This could include saving them the many weeks/months spent doing all the research themselves, saving money on other products in the future, referring to testimonials as proof that it works, etc. Like before, remember to use the limited-time discount as an incentive for them to take action now rather than later.

1 Day Delay

Email #7:

Give them **urgency** to grab your front-end product due to the new subscriber discount expiring soon, i.e. this is their last chance before they miss out on a great deal and achieving their goals. Also, share more results from other customers if you have them.

This sequence is specifically designed to overcome the major objections people face when presented with a buying opportunity: they aren't sure if you're knowledgeable on the topic or have experience in it, they need an extra incentive to avoid further delaying their purchase decision, they don't believe you, they need to know it worked for other people, they need emotional motivation, they need logical motivation, and they need a reason to take action immediately otherwise they'll suffer the "fear of loss."

After this sequence, you have two options:

Option A—if you have more than one front-end product to sell: Put them into another follow-up sequence (yes, it can follow this same format) for a *different* front-end product, if you have one.

Just be sure to start the new sequence with a different piece of valuable free content related to the paid offer being sold, as this prevents you as being seen as someone who hard sells *all* the time, and also provides value to the community—not to mention it demonstrates your expertise on the topic you're about to sell them a product on.

If you choose this option, you can have multiple sequences all leading on to each other, selling a different front-end product in each sequence.

For example:

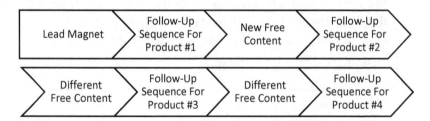

Then when you've ran out of products to promote, set up a trigger at the end of your sequences to add a tag to them called "broadcast" (or something similar of your choice). This labels them as somebody who has finished going through all these follow-up sequences and is ready to start receiving your regular "as and when" style emails, e.g. blog posts, latest content, recent news, etc.

So, when you send a regular email like this, you can send it to everyone who has the "broadcast" tag, and you'll know you won't be confusing and overwhelming the people who are currently in the follow-up sequences.

Or...

Option B—if you currently only have the one front-end product to sell: You can wrap up the follow-up sequence by setting a trigger at the end of it to add a tag to them called "broadcast" (or something similar of your choice) right away. As above, this labels them as somebody who has finished going through this follow-up sequence and is ready to start receiving your regular "as and when" style emails, e.g. blog posts, latest content, recent news, etc. So, with this option, essentially, you're just shortening down the follow-up sequence due currently to not having multiple products to sell (which is fine!).

Regarding how to set up these emails within your "autoresponder" / email list service, every service is different and it's tough to show every step in writing (which is why I have an entire video course which demonstrates these sorts of technical steps in a "do this, then do that" way). So, simply visit your email list service's help section to see their "how-to" guides. These will show you exactly how to use their service to achieve the above sequence(s). Plus, if you get confused, contact their support section—they're always available to guide you through it.

It may seem like extra work, but this process shouldn't take you any longer than an hour or two to set up, then it's done forever, and you'll be reaping the rewards of additional sales.

Once you've done it, congratulate yourself! Everything you've done before now is the most time-consuming and difficult part of starting a profitable online business, but fortunately you've learned a ton of new skills in the process which can be used again and again.

From here, it's all about acquiring customers for your products via the *Profit Process* you've set up.

STAGE 7: ACQUIRING CUSTOMERS

Most people think that getting "traffic" (marketing terminology for "website visitors") is the *holy grail* of making a huge profit online. Beginners often think, *If only I could get a million visitors, then I'd be rich!*—but the truth is you can find places that sell a service like that *right now* for $3. Just know that it would all be people who have no idea how they ended up on your site, with no results to come from it.

In reality, you can get traffic on tap from any advertising network, at any time. So, the holy grail isn't about the *quantity* of traffic, but instead about the *quality*—i.e. attracting the *right types* of people for your offer(s) and also making sure your *Profit Process resonates well enough* with people to make a positive return on any traffic costs and/or other investments.

But with that said, before we start with any kind of traffic strategy, you still need to be attracting the right people, at the right time of their journey, to the right web page, for the right offer.

So, how do you get traffic?

"Traffic" is generated when somebody is interested enough to visit your website.

For this to happen, this means traffic generation is simply a process of putting your message in front of people.

However, we've already established that quality is better than quantity, so hopefully you should be putting your message in front of *the right* people who would actually be *interested* in what you have to offer.

So, we need to find out where your ideal prospects hang out, then see if we can advertise there. That's traffic generation 101.

Note that this doesn't involve using some magic software to "generate a flood of traffic on demand." Traffic is not created from thin air, but instead as a result of putting a compelling message in front of the right people, so they click it to visit your website and find out more about what you have to offer them.

But before we can do this, we need to talk about something important that can make or break your advertising...

The 3 Major Levels Of Market Awareness

Traffic "quality" can be further defined by the level of *desire* and *buying intent*. The more *desire* for a solution (i.e. they *truly* want a problem fixed) and *intent* to buy (i.e. they're willing to *actually* follow through on that desire by *buying* something) your prospects have, the more sales you'll make.

Read that last paragraph again slowly, it's important.

Here's a handy diagram to illustrate this:

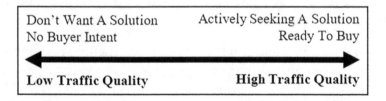

Once you understand this varying scale of traffic quality, you'll realize that traffic generation is *no longer* about getting as many people to your paid offer as possible (regardless of quality), but instead about converting the highest "quality" prospects possible from people who know nothing about you and your solution, into people who are ready to buy a solution based on your recommendation.

However, some audiences will require less persuading than others. Different niches and audiences will have different levels of awareness or "maturity" about their problems and solutions available to them.

An example of a **highly-aware or "mature" niche** would be the weight loss niche. People interested in weight loss are *aware* of the problem (e.g. "I'm unhappy with my body image and something needs to be done to fix it"), so they don't need to be educated about their issues, because they *already know*. Educating them about something they already know is not compelling to them, as it creates the "I already know this" mental opt out.

Plus, they also know there are tons of weight loss solutions out there, so selling something that simply promises they'll "lose weight" won't be compelling to them either, as they've heard it before.

So, in this niche, you'll need to position your marketing in a way that *assumes they already know* they need help, and also in a way that shows your offer as being different from your competitors' offers in some way *(covered earlier in this book when creating your products)*.

Whereas, an example of a niche with a **low level of maturity** would be when cryptocurrency was first created. People didn't have a clue what it was, how it worked, and there definitely weren't any "how-to" type products created around how to profit from it.

But soon enough, smart marketers took advantage of this new niche and created courses around it. Suddenly, these marketers didn't need to position their new products as unique in any kind of way, because there weren't many other products like it. They simply had to *inform* the marketplace of the product, and that was enough for most people to make a buying decision, as people didn't have any other buying options available to them.

Eventually, the niche was filled with more and more marketers selling more and more products, so it ascended to a high level of maturity pretty quickly.

In short, a prospect within a *more* mature niche requires *more* persuading and nurturing because they are more *skeptical* of the solution due to their previous purchases or other options available to them, i.e. "I've already tried this, and it didn't work for me," "how is your product different to his?" and so on.

In other words, a more mature niche means more skepticism, which means more persuading through a longer sales process. Whereas a prospect within a *less* mature niche requires *less* persuading because there are less buying objections created from previous purchases and a lack of other options available to them (i.e. they have no choice but to buy your product if they want a solution).

Obviously, the less mature niches don't stay like this for long, so you'll usually be working with a niche that is aware of their problem but is either:

a) *Unaware* of a solution—requires only a little selling and nurturing.

b) *Aware* of solutions—requires a moderate amount of selling and nurturing.

c) *Jaded* from trying many solutions and nothing working for them—requires a lot of selling and nurturing.

You can figure out which group your chosen niches fall into just by looking at your successful competitors' products and their sales processes. But nowadays for most markets, you're looking at your niche being in option (c). This is because most people have either failed before or are overwhelmed with the amount of solutions available to them.

We all know marketers love drawing pyramids, so here's one to illustrate my point for the more visual learners:

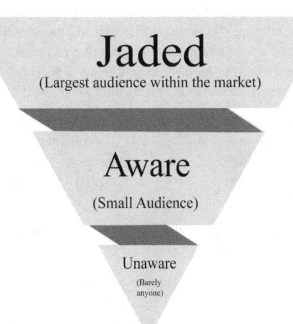

This means the job of your marketing is often to persuade *jaded* prospects to make a purchase, using logical and emotional evidence that matches their specific situation. Fortunately, this nurturing process doesn't take long—it can often happen in as few as 2-3 interactions with your advertising and subsequent marketing.

So, if you've tried making sales online before but failed spectacularly, it was probably because your advertisements weren't overcoming their skepticism and generating enough desire for your solution—and *you* as their chosen person to learn from—beforehand. This is especially true with higher priced products and services.

Think of it this way…

By sending people from a tiny advertisement straight to an affiliate offer's sales page, it's the equivalent of going into a gym and shouting, "Who wants to get HUGE muscles?!" at the top of your voice. Eventually you're going to get one or two people come to you out of desperation, but there's not exactly going to be a stampede of people rushing to buy stuff from you.

Another commonly-used example is asking someone to marry you on your first date. There's no relationship, no trust factor, nor any kind of concrete desire there. So, we need to develop that through your advertising and subsequent marketing.

The advertising is the initial introduction, and your marketing is everything after that.

We've already established that a follow-up sequence is the most effective way to scoop up these fence-sitters into your realm of influence, so you can persuade them to buy more from you, so fortunately you already have that in place.

Now you know the basics of what traffic generation involves (i.e. putting a message in front of your ideal prospects to generate a desire for them to check out your website) and adjusting your advertising message to match your niche's current level of market awareness, let's get into the most effective methods of driving traffic…

Most traffic methods can be broken down into two groups—free and paid. I should probably come up with a fancy name for these groups, but it is what it is.

Free traffic is usually people's first go-to because, well, it's free. However, the issue with free traffic methods is that they take a lot of effort to implement and a long time to start seeing any kind of results.

For example, one of the most effective free traffic strategies is content marketing. This involves writing blog posts or creating videos for either your own website, social media channels or other people's websites as a guest author, then getting them shared around the Internet due to the massive value the content provides to people.

However, this can be tough do to, because it takes around 2-5 hours to create a highly-valuable blog post or video (depending on the desired length of the content), then you have to find a popular website that will accept your content and share it with their subscribers.

But if you're lucky enough to do all that, their subscribers will click the links to your website where referenced within the content and/or at the end of it, then check out what you have to offer.

Another free traffic method involves finding popular forums within your niche, creating a profile and adding a link to your website in the "signature" section of that profile, then replying to people's posts with valuable advice. When your reply appears in the forum, your signature appears below it, containing a link back to your website. So, if people like your reply and find it valuable, they'll often click your link in your signature to learn more from you.

But again, this method isn't perfect because it takes a very long time to build up the amount of posts you have in the forum, and therefore an even longer time to get any kind of noticeable traffic from this method.

A variation of this method is "infiltrating" groups on social media sites, such as Facebook groups. Simply provide as much value as possible, then provide recommendations to learn more about your topic at your website where relevant. But again, this is very time-consuming and not that scalable.

Another "free" traffic method is Search Engine Optimization, i.e. getting ranked higher in the search results for the phrases your ideal prospects search for in search engines (although people usually focus on Google and Bing). I say it's a "free" traffic method (in quotes) because it's actually *pseudo-free* and takes a very long time to achieve sustainable rankings in the search results. This is because you can either spend hours and hours building up backlinks to your website in the right places without getting some kind of "slap" from the search engines or do what most people do and *hire* an SEO expert to do the work for you. If you're hiring someone, then you may as well just be paying for the traffic directly instead of hoping someone else is going to get you some kind of tangible results—and that's if the search engines don't change their rules again in a few months after doing all your hard work.

I don't know about you, but personally I don't like the idea of spending hours of hard work on something with *the hope* of some level of traffic coming in—not to mention that these methods aren't easily scaled (i.e. going from a small amount of traffic to a large amount), and you aren't really in control of your results.

Don't get me wrong—a lot of online companies have become successful by driving traffic through content marketing, SEO and other methods, but they'll happily tell you how much work was involved to achieve that.

In other words, you're essentially trading your sweat equity for traffic.

So, because I like to keep the hard work to a minimum and instead focus on building a mostly-automated business that gives me a better lifestyle, I personally prefer paid traffic methods, as this allows you to be in direct control of how much traffic you receive, with just 10 minutes of work. You can literally click a few buttons to create an advertising campaign and start getting as much traffic as you want within an hour.

And if the price of getting traffic is a concern for you, consider this… Most marketers often complain about high or rising traffic costs, however if your traffic is costing you a seemingly high amount of $3 per click/visitor, but your *Profit Process* is fine-tuned enough to convert those visitors into paying customers to the equivalent of $5 per click/visitor, then the last time I checked, $5 – $3 = $2, so you therefore have a $2 *profit* per click/visitor and have nothing to worry about. It's all relative.

Paid traffic isn't about throwing money into some big black hole and *hoping* for good results. It's all measured so precisely that you can *engineer* a positive return on your advertising spend.

This mindset is the difference between having a hobby business and a wildly successful business.

People who are scared to learn how to make paid traffic work for them will fall back to free traffic methods that only provide a trickle of traffic here and there, making sales unpredictably, resulting in the business being a hobby. And a hobby business will provide a hobby income.

And funnily enough, these people won't hesitate to spend an extra $3,000+ on more courses and training programs but spending money on traffic is "too expensive" for them.

Whereas the entrepreneurs who aren't scared of a challenge to change their entire life for the better will master paid traffic within a week or two, then have the skills to generate a profit on demand at any scale—whether it's four figures per month, five figures per month, and beyond.

So, I'll leave that decision up to you. However, I can say with 100% certainty that if I had never learned how to use paid traffic, my business would *still* be sitting at around $1,000 or so per month right now, instead of at $50,000-$70,000+ per month like it is now.

Ready?

Paid traffic is all about finding a company that has an existing audience and paying them money to put your message in front of them.

Then to make a positive return from that investment, you need to create an ad that resonates with your audience, and that ad needs to be shown in the right place to reach the right people. People who don't think about these things usually end up losing money, then end up complaining on a forum somewhere that paid traffic doesn't work for them.

There are a few ways you can do this…

The first way is to find marketers who already have a responsive email list in your niche, then ask them if they'd be open to sending an email promoting your offer to their subscribers. This email is known as a "solo ad," as it should be the *only* advertisement in that email, compared to having lots of other focuses within the email.

These solo ads are easier to come by in some niches over others, but this works with any niche that contains digital products being sold. After all, if they have a customer base acquired from purchases of their product, then they also have an email list for those customers that you can pay to be put in front of.

For example, the "Internet marketing" / "make money online" niche is filled with solo ad sellers who actually have dedicated sales pages for their solo ad services, explaining how it works, their different pricing pages for a guaranteed number of "clicks" (marketing terminology for "website visitors," as these people will be clicking your link in their email), and so on. A good directory for this is www.SoloAdsX.com.

But other niches like weight loss aren't as knowledgeable about this method, so you may need to explain this to them, asking them something like this:

"Hi, I have a valuable offer your subscribers would like and benefit from, and I wondered if you'd be open to sending one email to your newsletter about it, and I'll pay you a reasonable amount of money before you send the email to do it?"

This way, the marketer thinks, "One email and I get paid whether my people buy or not? I have nothing to lose!" Then if they ask for more details, you can simply negotiate pricing to do so.

There are also broker sites dedicated to solo ads for niches outside of "Internet marketing," such as www.NextMark.com.

For most niches, generally, you should be looking to pay between $0.30 to $0.60 per click, depending on the quality of the traffic. If it's going to be sent to an email list solely consisting of customers, you can expect to pay upwards of $1 per click, depending on how aware the marketer is of their list's true value—but of course your sales will be much higher as a result, so it works out in your favor.

You may not know how much traffic (i.e. how many "clicks") they can send beforehand, so it's good practice to ask them how many clicks they get for each broadcast email on average, then negotiate the lowest price you can get from there.

Once they agree, you can write an email promoting your stuff (or let them write it—it's up to you), then send it over to them with the payment. Then it's just a matter of waiting until they send the email broadcast and analyzing the results.

I used solo ads to grow my business from zero to around $5,000 net profit per month (after which I moved onto a different traffic strategy we'll talk about next), and during this time I learned some important lessons:

1) Always ask about how the marketer's email list was built. Their subscribers should have actually opted in themselves (instead of being imported by the marketer without the subscribers' permission) and be emailed at least once per week to keep their responsiveness as high as possible.

2) You should test whether it works best to send people straight to your sales page, or to your squeeze page. Some marketers won't be happy with sending their subscribers to a sales page for a paid product, so you'll be forced to have their traffic sent to your squeeze page—which is not a bad thing, as this allows you to build your audience while following up with the non-buyers, too. But sending your traffic straight to the sales page will work better in some niches, and you'll make more sales sending people to free stuff via your squeeze

page first in other niches. So, it's all about testing what works best for you, your niche, and your offer.

3) Always create a tracking link for the link you're promoting, so you can see how many clicks you've gotten and ideally how many new subscribers and sales, too. For example, www.bit.ly is a free service that allows you to see how many clicks you've gotten, but a tracking service like ClickMagick will allow you to track how many subscribers and sales as well. This way, you can track your subscribers and sales, then see a return on your investment to get the traffic in the first place. I'd recommend creating a separate tracking link for each solo ad seller, so you can see who is performing best.

4) If a solo ad seller gets you good results, go back to them for another round! Keep milking that ROI until it dries up, then go back to them a month or two later to do the same thing again.

5) Some more shady solo ad sellers will redirect their traffic from other places to your link, meaning those people have no idea why they've landed on your website and your conversion rates are often rock bottom as a result. I usually ask if they are going to do this before placing my order, as I prefer my prospects to know *exactly* what they're getting *before* they visit my website, as the conversion rates throughout my *Profit Process* are always much higher this way.

6) It's usually good to keep a spreadsheet of the solo ad sellers you've ordered from, when they're going to be sending the traffic, how many clicks you've received so far, the opt-in rate from their traffic, the number of sales from their traffic, and so on. This helps to keep

everything organized when you're buying from multiple people at the same time.

Generally, solo ad traffic does work well—especially when you've built up a collection of solo ad sellers who always get good results for you, as you can just keep cycling through them. As I mentioned, I built my business from scratch to $5,000 net profit per month just using this traffic generation method alone.

However, it took me a lot of sifting through different solo ad sellers to get to this point, as your results will vary massively from one seller to another. It's a risk worth taking if you're in this for the long run, but personally, I disliked having the same discussion over and over again with every solo ad seller as if I was living through the *Groundhog Day* movie, and also the long waiting times for the traffic to start coming in—only for half of your solo ads to end in a net loss.

That's when I started investigating other paid traffic sources and focused on one method which I still use to this very day—"PPC" (pay-per-click) advertising networks. I use the term "PPC" loosely, as nowadays these networks have way more possibilities than just paying for clicks, but we'll leave that discussion for another time. So, let's call them advertising networks.

The most popular of these advertising networks are Google Ads, Facebook Ads, and Bing Ads. There *are* bigger platforms like Advertising.com, but for the beginner entrepreneur, these three networks are the best to start with.

Bing Ads has the smallest learning curve of them all, but also the least amount of traffic. I also feel its display algorithm (i.e. its mechanism to show your ads to the right people) isn't as good as the other two networks, too. However, if you're not able to use the other two networks for some reason, this is a good network to try out.

But personally, because of Bing's small amount of traffic, I prefer to use the other two—Google Ads (previously known as Google AdWords) and Facebook Ads.

It's pretty overwhelming to learn how to use *both* networks effectively and manage everything at the same time, so I'd recommend choosing just one of them to start with.

My go-to for my own ads *and* new clients is always Facebook Ads, as this network always results in the best ROI and is typically easiest to master. Plus, you've most likely used Facebook before, so you'll probably already be familiar with how posts get displayed on there. So that's what we'll be focusing on in this book, as that's where I can provide the most value from my millions of dollars spent on ads across my own campaigns and clients' campaigns.

But before you do anything, you need to make sure your ads will be *compliant* with your chosen advertising network's guidelines, so your account doesn't get banned and leave you up the creek without a paddle.

When I first started out, I was selling other people's products as an affiliate. "The simplest solution is the best!" I thought. So, I just copied and pasted my affiliate link for a hypey offer with a ton of claims into a Google AdWords ad (this was before they rebranded to Google Ads, and also before I knew that creating your own products was way more profitable) and waited for the commissions to roll in.

At first, their automated system approved my ad. I was getting hundreds of people clicking my ad and checking out the offer, yet no sales whatsoever. *Why is nobody buying?!?* I thought, frustrated.

Little did I know that this strategy was also against Google's advertising guidelines due to the huge claims being made on the paid offer's sales page, so I got my account banned after it was reviewed by a human three days later, after spending hundreds of dollars with no sales to show for it.

So, don't make the same mistake!

I'm not saying you can't make any kind of claim (e.g. "lose 30 pounds," "make six figures," etc.) in your offers, as most sales copy is in fact based around the *results* you can get for people. That's why people buy—because they want the results you promise.

But what *I am* saying is that you have to be strategic in the way you advertise it.

So, which page you send your traffic to depends on how *compliant* your niche and offer is with your chosen advertising network's policies and guidelines. This means you should read your chosen network's advertising guidelines from beginning to end *before* doing anything, then revisit the parts of it you feel your sales page may be in violation of.

If the sales page you'd like to promote is in violation of any one of the parts of the guidelines, worry not! Most experts will tell you to change your niche to something more compliant, but personally I feel you should always follow your passion, whatever it is—and there are always ways to do that (as long as it's a legal topic, of course).

So, in this case, you have two options:

a) Create a separate version of your sales page which *is* compliant with the advertising networks' guidelines (usually containing less/no claims, and generally being less hypey) and promote that instead, or…

b) Send your traffic to your squeeze page for your free lead magnet—which of course then leads into your sales page after people opt in, as we discussed earlier in this book.

Out of the two options, option (b) is usually easiest to start with, to be done while you work on option (a). However, I do feel that option (b) is only a temporary solution and is pretty risky to do in the long term.

For example, the Facebook Ads policies really hate anything that's "make money online," "MLM" or "business opportunities." Any time you mention the phrase "make money" or "work from home," you'll usually get your account banned right away. Plus, if you're in that niche, your sales pages will logically mention income claims and how the extra money is going to influence people's lives for the better—because that's what the customers in that niche are looking for.

So, as a workaround, you'll need to send your traffic to a squeeze page which promotes a free product that isn't directly related to making money, but instead focuses on a *smaller* part of the whole system.

A good way to decide this is to map out your *ideal* prospect's journey to their big end goal and focus on just one of the steps required to get there.

In my case, my "online business" niche is too similar to the "make money online" niche for Facebook's liking (even though it's more business-focused and way less scammy), so for the last six years I've had to send my advertisements to a squeeze page promoting a lead magnet called "The 12 Profitable Niches To Build An Online Business Around," as choosing a profitable niche is a smaller part of their bigger goal to make a profit online. Logically, if they're interested in finding a niche for an online business, then they'll want to know how to make money with it. Problem solved.

> *Sidenote*: Notice that it says, "online business," because if I'd have said "to make money with," this is non-compliant, and I'd have had my account shut down by now. I know that because that's what I did, twice! Fortunately, I finally learned my lesson on my third try.

Because the topic is about finding niches and not making money, it suddenly makes a non-compliant niche compliant, even though the pages after that may not be 100% compliant if I were to advertise them directly with Facebook Ads.

But, if you're in a niche that is in fact 100% compliant with the paid traffic networks' guidelines (e.g. meditation, survival skills, etc.) and you don't make any outrageous ("unrealistic") claims, then you're good to start advertising with them.

Again—to be 100% clear with this—every single word of copy on your sales page must be compliant with the advertising guidelines of your chosen traffic network. If it makes an unrealistic claim or talks about something in the policies that isn't allowed to be talked about, you're eventually going to get your account shut down—even if it's approved by their automated system initially. So, be sure to check this thoroughly, as the networks not only review your ad, but also the page you're sending traffic to, too.

In this case, you would advertise your product, sending people directly to the sales page for it.

Once you've identified which will be the best path for you, it's time to create your ad campaign.

There are three main stages to getting your new ads account set up: Initiation, Track, and Launch.

Stage #1: Initiation

This stage is all about laying the groundwork for your ads account to function, and fortunately only needs to be done once, ever.

Your first step is to create your Facebook Ads account, which can be done by first creating a Business Manager account at https://business.facebook.com, then going to your business settings and creating an ad account.

If you already have an ads account, you should link it to this new Business Manager account too, as it helps to minimize any red flags of "suspicious activity" within your account, which if left unchecked can lead to an account suspension (for some weird reason).

You should also create a Facebook Page for your company, as this will be linked to your ads. I'd recommend creating the page around your personal brand (i.e. "James Francis" rather than "Digital Prosperity") here—even if you're using company branding. This is because social media is all about people connecting with people, and ads ran from personal-branded pages typically get better results than those ran from a company-branded page. Yep, I've tested it. The only exception to this rule is if you're in a B2B market that requires company professionalism—but even then, feel free to test this for yourself if you're unsure.

I know you're probably eager to get started, but there's one last piece of housekeeping before you start setting up your ads. Go to your Business Settings once again, then go to the section which contains your payment details, then add a payment method to your account. This is where your ad spend will be billed to, so make sure there are always enough funds in the account to avoid problems in the future.

I'd recommend avoiding the PayPal option if presented with it, as this can lead to a whole host of information mismatches between your Facebook and PayPal accounts, which again can get your Facebook Ads account shut down for "suspicious activity" (i.e. suspected fraud).

Phew! Now we can actually get started with setting up your ads campaign.

Stage #2: Track

Once you're inside your ads account, you'll need to open the top navigation menu and select the link to set up your advertising pixel. Currently this is named as "Pixels" in the "Measure & Report" column. However, Facebook are changing this all the time, so the wording doesn't matter—just look for something that says "Pixels" or similar if it's been moved.

On that page, just name your pixel whatever you want (but naming it after your company would be a good idea) and copy and paste the tracking code you're given on every web page of your website. Fortunately, you only need to do this once but doing so allows you to track the results from your ads—instead of operating blindly based on the hand-selected stats that Facebook gives you.

Next, I'd recommend going to Custom Audiences within the top navigation menu and creating the following three audiences, with the following parameters:

1) **Name:** "Prospect – Visited Squeeze Page"
   URL to enter in the field: Contains: The URL of your squeeze page.
   My explanation: Eventually you'll want to show

different ads to people who clicked on your ad(s) for your lead magnet but didn't opt in, so setting this up now helps you to build up an audience to be used in the future.

2) **Name:** "Lead – [Name Of Lead Magnet]" *(Obviously change this accordingly).*
URL to enter in the field: Contains: The URL of the page shown immediately after people sign up for your lead magnet, which should hopefully be the page which gives them what they signed up for, a short explanation about the limited-time incentive to buy now rather than later, and the sales page for your front-end product below it.
My explanation: Doing this will allow you to exclude this audience from any lead generation campaigns, because you don't want to show ads about signing up to your free lead magnet to people who have *already* signed up for it.

3) **Name:** "Sale – [Name Of Product]" *(Again, obviously replace this accordingly).*
URL to enter in the field: Contains: The URL of the page shown immediately after people purchase the product.
My explanation: This allows you to exclude your buyers from your ad campaigns, as you don't want to show your ads about a paid product they've already bought. Be sure to do this for every product you're selling in your *Profit Process* and elsewhere on your website.

There are many more audiences you can create, such as people who have visited your order form, people who have visited blog posts on specific topics (so you can show ads to them about products related to those topics), and much more. But let's keep it simple for now to avoid feeling overwhelmed.

Next, you'll want to mimic these audiences within the "Custom Conversions" section of the top navigation menu. Literally copy them in exactly the same way with the exact same parameters. You'll just want to set the "Visited Squeeze Page" custom conversion in the "View Content" category, the "Lead" custom conversion in the "Lead" category, and the "Sale" custom conversions in the "Purchase" category—just so Facebook reports your data correctly.

There are plenty more *advanced* ways of setting up this tracking, including:

- Having the currency converted automatically for you if the currency of your ads account is different from the currency in which your products are sold.
- If a new customer reloads the order confirmation page three times, it'll normally report it as three sales instead of one, but we can do some advanced coding to have the code only report back to Facebook one time per customer.
- Add somebody to a custom audience when they reach specific parts of your email follow-up sequence, so your ads can mimic the flow of that.
- Report a conversion after people spend a specific amount of time on the page, or when they click a specific button or link on your page.
- … And a ton more cool (yet nerdy!) stuff.

However, I didn't intend this book to be about programming and coding, so I'll leave those advanced tracking methods for another time.

Once you've set up your pixel, custom audiences and custom conversions (what I like to call "the conversion trifecta"), you're free to start creating the ads themselves.

Stage #3: Launch

Before you create your ad campaign, I'd recommend going through Facebook's help section (currently at https://www.facebook.com/business/help) to get you familiar with the Ads Manager interface, what the buttons do, and so on.

Once you've done that, you'll know that Facebook Ads has three main "levels" of ad creation:

- Campaign
  - Ad Set
    - Ad

Typically, I'll have one campaign for each offer I'm promoting, so this usually means we create just one campaign for a new client (until they create more offers, anyway).

In most cases, you'll want to set this campaign's conversion objective (located in the settings for it) to conversions. Not "traffic," but *conversions*—as that's primarily what you want.

This tells Facebook's algorithm to prioritize showing your ads to people who have proven themselves to take action, instead of just clicking on the ads and closing the page right away. This alone will bump up your results compared to what most advertisers do.

Inside this campaign, you'll want to create one ad set per audience you want to target. This allows you to get separate statistics for each ad set (and therefore each audience), so you can see which audiences are working well for you and which aren't, therefore allowing you to shut off the losers and scale the winners.

But initially, create just *one* ad set which you can duplicate later to save yourself a whole bunch of extra work.

Within this ad set's settings, you'll want to follow these 10 commandments, working down from the top:

1) If you're able to send your traffic straight to the sales page, set the website conversion event to the Custom Conversion you created for purchases of your front-end paid offer **OR** if you're forced to promote the squeeze page due to compliance issues on your sales page, set it to the Lead Custom Conversion event you created.

2) Set the daily budget to a minimum of $10 per day (or 10 of whatever your currency is, e.g. 10 GBP). Anything less than this, and the advertising algorithm will have a hard time finding the right people for you due to not having enough data to do that. I usually set this to $20 per day, as you can turn off the ads at any time if needed.

3) In the Custom Audiences section, exclude all the Sale Custom Conversions you created if you're sending traffic straight to the sales page (as you don't want to show ads to people who've already purchased), **and** also exclude the Lead Custom Conversion you created if you're sending traffic to your squeeze page (again, you don't want to be showing your ads to people who've already signed up for the thing you're showing them ads for).

4) I usually start by setting the locations as the "big 6": United States, United Kingdom, Ireland, Canada, New Zealand, and Australia. You can then see which countries perform best when analyzing the results of

your ad after you start gaining some traction and take out the losers if necessary.

5) Same principle with the age setting—initially set it fairly broad at 25—65+, then you can narrow down the age groups based on your results.

6) Same principle with the gender setting—initially set it to "All," unless you're in a niche that is focused solely on one gender (e.g. helping female entrepreneurs).

7) Language(s) is obvious—set it to English, unless your website is primarily in another language, of course.

8) In the "Detailed Targeting" section, I usually start with just one interest that my ideal prospects would be following which has above 500,000 people in it. Anything less than that, and you'll start running into issues with your ads getting saturated too quickly, and the algorithm will have a hard time finding a responsive audience for you.

9) In the "Placements" section, I usually start with just Facebook News Feed, as this is typically the easiest to make a positive ROI with. You can always expand it later.

10) Be sure to check the "only when connected to Wi-Fi" box for mobile devices, as people freak out if your high file size videos start playing on their data plan.

Now, this isn't a "be all and end all"—it's just a basis to start your testing. That's because advertising is ALL about testing what works best for you, your company, your niche, your offer and your audience. If you start out with the above, you can—and should—tweak your targeting settings based on the initial results you get from your ad.

Within this ad set, I'd recommend creating three different variations of your ads. Try to make them as different as possible, as this way you'll increase your chances of the statistics being different to each other and finding a winning ad. So be creative!

Once I've created the three ad variations, I'll usually go back to the Ad Set view and duplicate the ad set to have a total of five ad sets, each with a different "interest" I want to test.

So, I have—and you should have—five ad sets, three ads in each, totaling 15 different combinations.

Advanced Tip: If you publish the three original ads first before duplicating them, you can get the Ad ID number for each one (shown at the top when editing each specific ad), then you can use this Ad ID number when creating an ad in the "Use Existing Post" option. Just click the "Enter Post ID" link and paste it in the box. This allows your ads to retain their social proof (likes, shares, etc.) across your different ad sets, instead of being reset to zero for each ad set.

I'll usually start off by creating three text and image-based ads, then once I find a winner, I'll create a video version of it and see whether the text or video version works better. From there, it's all about testing new ideas, checking the results, and repeating the process until your ads are generating a positive ROI.

But for this to happen, you'll need to show all your statistics instead of just the hand-picked ones Facebook shows you by default. So, click in the "columns" dropdown menu and select "Performance and Clicks," then do it again but select "Customize Columns."

(Again, the wording may change, so follow the same principle if this happens.)

From the huge list of additional statistics, I'll usually go to the "Custom Conversions" section in the left menu, then select the option to show sales of my front-end product—regardless of whether I'm sending traffic straight there or to your squeeze page. I'd also recommend checking the box under "Purchases" → "Value" to show the actual sales figures across all your products within your *Profit Process*. Hit the save button and you're good to go.

After doing this, go to the Columns menu again to save this setting as a default setting, saving you having to go through this same process every time you open up your Ads Manager.

This gives you the full picture of your results instead of just a snapshot.

However, all of these metrics can be fairly confusing to begin with, so I'd recommend hovering over the column titles to learn more about each one. But ideally, after 500 impressions (called "Reach" in the table of statistics), your ad should have a minimum of these statistics:

- 5% CTR (All)
- 1.5% CTR (Link)
- 8/10 Relevance Score

If your ad isn't reaching these minimum numbers, then it's going to be tough to sustain your ads without costs increasing quickly, and also make any kind of profit. But luckily, these numbers depend entirely on *you* and how compelling your ads are to people, which is a good thing because it means you can *improve* them by testing different variations of your ad.

Some ads will reach way beyond these figures right out of the gate, whereas others will be way below. This is totally down to you and how good your ad campaign is.

However, not everyone is going to buy straight away, so we can "scoop up" the people who don't take the action you want them to take with retargeting ads.

This feature is in both Google Ads and Facebook Ads, and it allows you to show a different ad to people who've taken a desired action, like visited a specific website URL, clicked a specific button on your website, and so on. This is known as "retargeting." If you've been followed around the web by an ad after visiting a specific web page, then you've probably experienced this yourself from the position of being their prospect. It can be annoying when done without much creativity and logical thought, but it's incredibly effective from a marketer's standpoint when done correctly.

Using this retargeting functionality, you should "retarget" those nonbuyers by showing a *different* ad promoting your free lead magnet (i.e. your squeeze page) to *people who visit your sales page but don't visit the order form* to buy on their first visit.

Think of it like this...

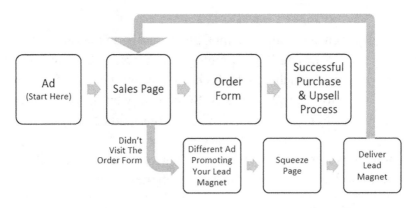

Within the Facebook Ads network, this is accomplished by creating a custom audience called something like "Prospects—Visited Sales Page But Didn't Buy," then setting the rule as:

- Visited this URL:
  https://www.yourwebsite.com/yoursalespage
- Didn't visit this URL:
  https://www.yourwebsite.com/salespageforyourfirst upsell

(Obviously replacing the URLs with your own URLs accordingly.)

… Then creating an ad with its audience set to this new custom audience with the above rules applied.

Advanced Tip: We're not using the "order confirmation" page URL in the "didn't visit" part of the audience rules, as some people close the browser window before reaching the order confirmation page and those people therefore wouldn't be included in the custom audience. So, it's better to use the URL for the web page shown immediately after they become a customer, which should be the sales page for your first upsell.

By focusing your ad campaign primarily on the **sale** rather than the lead, you'll be training the advertising network's algorithm (the machine which chooses which people see your ads) to only show your ads to people who have proven themselves to *buy* products similar to your paid offer.

This is super important, as every one of my clients' failing campaigns were getting traffic which has proven itself to opt in, but *not* to buy—and that was the reason they were failing.

Think of it this way...

If you're promoting a free lead magnet on a squeeze page and you set that as the objective of your ad campaign, the algorithm is going to do its best to find people for you who have proven themselves to be good at signing up for *free* content—not necessarily *buying* products.

Whereas if you set the objective to a purchase of a specific product, the algorithm will find you people most likely to *purchase* your product.

That's why it's often best to send people straight to the sales page for your product if possible, as you'll be acquiring the highest quality traffic with proven buying intent. Then the people you retarget with your lead magnet will still be more predisposed to buying rather than setting the original objective as "leads" (i.e. people who are most likely to opt in for free stuff).

However, this isn't always possible due to compliance reasons, so you'll need to choose which option works best for you here.

To do this, you can create another ad set with no interest targeting, just *including* the audience of the people who've visited your squeeze page, but *excluding* your Custom

Audiences containing your customers and leads. Then create an ad sending them to a different lead magnet or use different ad copy that persuades them to sign up for the same lead magnet a second time around.

Another method to boost your ROI is creating another ad set which *includes* a Custom Audience of people who have visited your sales page and *excludes* a Custom Audience of people who visited the order form and all the audiences of your customers. Then create an ad with different ad copy to generate enough of a desire within the prospect to actually start the order process. This ad can send people either directly to the same sales page as before, a different sales page with a different marketing angle or content format, or straight to the order form. For us, reminding people of the limited-time discount often works best, but test it and see what works best for you!

A final method I'd recommend using is creating another separate ad set which *includes* a Custom Audience of people who visited the order form, but *excludes* the Custom Audiences containing your customers. Then simply write some ad copy going over some common objections to buying, sending them back to the order form.

These three retargeting ads alone will boost your ROI by a noticeable amount, when done correctly with the right copy. But your creativity is your only limit here, so feel free to test different ideas and see what gets you the best results.

Following the process in this chapter will give you one main ad campaign to acquire new customers, and another (your "retargeting" campaign) to "scoop up" the people who didn't take action the first time around.

From here on, it's about focusing on this primary traffic method to improve your ads and *Profit Process* until you get a positive ROI.

The first time you read through this chapter, it may seem overwhelming to you with all the technical terminology if you're a self-confessed technophobe. So, I'd recommend re-reading this chapter when you're at a computer/laptop and actually following along with it, step-by-step.

Then if you *still* feel you need some help with this, feel free to contact us at https://support.digitalprosperity.com and we'll be happy to find either a Facebook Ads training program or "done for you" type solution that works best for you.

Aside from Facebook Ads, it's also a good idea to have other traffic streams in place, especially when they generate a high ROI like the ones I'm about to reveal to you. Consider these traffic methods a way to capture the "low hanging fruit" on the side.

The first method you can add to your arsenal is to contact other product owners and see if they'd be willing to accept a flat monthly payment to have a small ad for your product's sales page on their order confirmation page, in a "recommended products" section or something similar.

People who have just completed a purchase successfully and reached an order confirmation page are *so* much more likely to make another purchase, compared to the people just sitting around on Facebook.

This works especially well if you have some kind of "free plus shipping" type offer, where the product you're selling is free but you're asking them to pay to have it shipped to them, e.g. a book like this one, or a small physical item costing you less than \$10-\$15 in hard costs. Alternatively, a free trial for one of your best products works well too.

This works so well because you can position the offer as a "free bonus" for them becoming a new customer, which tends to get more attention than "check out this other recommended offer that will cost you more money."

But if the product owners aren't too keen on receiving a flat monthly fee for them doing this, they may be more responsive to selling your product as an affiliate there on the order confirmation page—and in their customer follow-up sequence—instead. Give them a large commission (hopefully 100%) for the front-end offer, then 50% commissions on all the upsells. This is usually enough to incentivize people, as they think, "100% commissions!? That's like having my own product!" then you make the profit from the upsells and future promotions to those customers you've acquired at no upfront cost to you.

However, this does require you to have some kind of affiliate program set up and in place to accurately track and pay their commissions, which could take a few hours to set up—but would be more than worth it if you're receiving a trickle of sales every month on autopilot.

Another method is to approach other product owners in your niche and ask them if they'd be willing to do a cross-promotion with you. This essentially involves you promoting their product to your email list as an affiliate, then they do the same for your product. It can be at the same scheduled time or staggered to avoid any suspicion—it's up to you. However, like the above method, this does require you to have some kind of affiliate program set up and in place.

Now you have plenty of methods to get traffic—and customers—for your website and products, you'll either be getting poor results or amazing results. Either way, your next step is to be optimizing your advertising and *Profit Process* to get the highest ROI possible.

STAGE 8: OPTIMIZATION

At this point, you'll have *some* kind of results—good or bad. Often around 80% of your campaigns won't work as intended, and the remaining 20% will be a winner right out of the gate. The good old 80/20 rule.

What most inexperienced entrepreneurs do when they get bad results is get all emotional, declare that the system they're following "doesn't work" and throw in the towel, losing all their time, effort and money invested. The sad truth is that the profit they're looking for is just a few tweaks away at this stage, but they don't know this yet, so they then start something new and repeat the cycle.

But of course, you're smarter than that, right?

Instead, if things didn't go as planned, you need to *analyze* your results (i.e. WHY it didn't work out as planned, specifically) and *optimize* any failing parts of the system, then repeat.

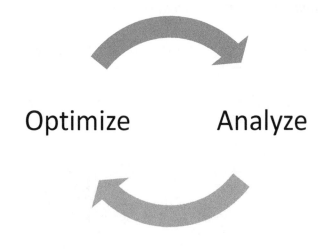

Optimize   Analyze

After all, the system doesn't just contain one element that works or doesn't work—it's comprised of multiple different elements that follow on from each other and have to all work together.

Because they're all connected and some web pages are more compelling to people than others, just one failing element can affect your results for everything else in your *Profit Process* too, causing a bottleneck. Therefore, when most people get terrible results, it's often because something isn't as compelling as it should be at the very beginning of their *Profit Process*, which is affecting everything else that comes after it. See how that works?

Fortunately, we can find the details of how well each page works ("converts") from analytics services such as Google Analytics, or right in the "Stats" area of your ClickFunnels account.

Here's an example of a failing *Profit Process* before being optimized...

(Continued on the next page...)

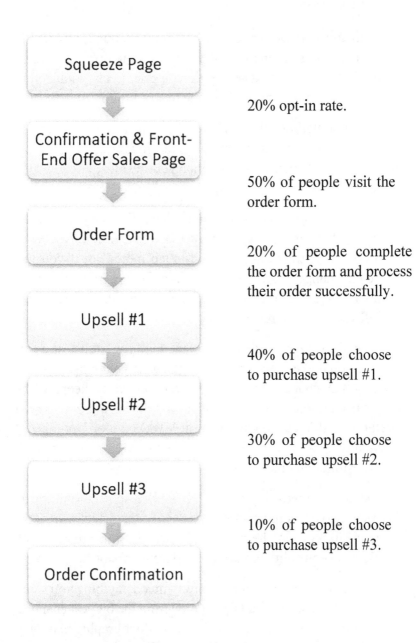

Squeeze Page

20% opt-in rate.

Confirmation & Front-End Offer Sales Page

50% of people visit the order form.

Order Form

20% of people complete the order form and process their order successfully.

Upsell #1

40% of people choose to purchase upsell #1.

Upsell #2

30% of people choose to purchase upsell #2.

Upsell #3

10% of people choose to purchase upsell #3.

Order Confirmation

Now we have all the data in front of us, we can identify that the squeeze page only having a 20% opt-in rate is restricting the amount of leads going through the funnel.

However, if we test a new headline, product graphic, bio section or similar to increase the opt-in rate to 40% (i.e. where it should be for most niches), then you effectively double your results—and sales—throughout the rest of your *Profit Process.*

And sometimes that's all it takes—just a small tweak to your copy on the page, the page design or layout, or the marketing angle you're using—then your results jump to match your expectations.

However, there are many things that influence your results, including the time of day, day of the week, time of the year, traffic quality, traffic source, and much more. So, if you just make the change to the current version of the page, it isn't a fair comparison to your previous results, as these other things could be influencing your results too.

That's why it's super important that you split test every change you make. This involves duplicating your existing page, making the change on that new version while keeping the original page the same, then using a split testing software (I prefer Visual Website Optimizer at VWO.com or Optimizely) to equally split your traffic between the two versions and track your desired outcome for you.

Hence the term "split test," as you're splitting the traffic between two or more versions of a page to test which works the best, by looking at the results of each version after enough traffic has been split between the different versions.

Although you can split test pretty much anything you want, the biggest boosts in results will come from the biggest changes. For example, split testing a different product graphic may only get you a small increase in sales, but split testing a completely different marketing angle for your sales copy can massively increase your sales—from the same quantity of traffic.

That's ultimately what this is about. Trying to create the best possible version of your page to squeeze as many results as possible out of your traffic. Here's why…

1000 visitors X 1% conversion rate = 10 sales = $270 in sales for a $27 product.

1000 visitors X 6% conversion rate = 60 sales = $1,620 in sales for the same $27 product.

Yep—that's from the same amount of traffic.

Here are my "go-to" elements to test for a brand new sales page:

1) The price of the product. Sometimes a low $27 price will get you more net profit than a higher price of $47 due to more front-end sales and therefore more customers buying products from the upsell sequence.

2) The marketing angle of the sales copy. For example, try focusing on different main benefits of the products to see which appeals most to your customers. What do they *really* want?

3) The first 500 words of the sales page, which copywriters call the "lead in." This is what hooks people into reading the rest of the page or closing the window altogether, so it has the most impact on your results above everything else.

4) Graphics and general page design. Whenever I've hired a graphic designer trained in direct response marketing to make the page more visually appealing, it's increased my sales every time. So, now it's standard procedure after we know an offer is resonating with people. Definitely worth the one-time flat fee investment.

5) Adding more buy buttons throughout the sales page vs. just at the end. When people need more persuading, typically leaving the buy buttons until the bottom of the page works better, but sometimes your prospects are more ready to buy than you think, which is when scattering them throughout your page in relevant places helps to boost your sales.

There are plenty more ideas you can test, and this testing process is only limited by your own creativity.

These small split tests can—and should—be done to every step of your *Profit Process*, and also to your advertising campaigns too.

For advertising campaigns, you'll want to test (in this order):

1) Different images for your ad. Try to make them as different as possible.

2) Adding a short video ad vs. the winning static image from the previous test.

3) Your main ad copy.

4) Your ad's headline (usually below the image for Facebook Ads).

5) Your ad's CTA button (e.g. "Learn More," "Download," "Sign Up," etc.).

6) Your ad's description (usually below the headline for Facebook Ads).

Fortunately, this becomes pretty easy to do with the use of the "Dynamic Creative" option within your ad set's settings. Just turn it on, then you can create multiple variations of the same ad. Just keep in mind that the more variations you have running at the same time, the more traffic—and therefore advertising budget—you'll need to find the winners.

Once you've found the winners and have optimized every step in your *Profit Process* to get a positive ROI, it's simply a matter of scaling your advertising campaign in three main ways:

- **Method #1 is "budget scaling"**—to increase the daily budget on each ad set. Although it's tempting to make huge leaps in budget here (like going from $20 per day to $1000 per day in the hopes of buying a private jet next week), the key is to do it gradually, otherwise the advertising algorithm won't know what to do and will reduce your results in a big way. So, if you're starting at $20 per day, instead of going straight to $200 per day, change it first to $30 per day, wait three days, then to $50 per day, wait three days, then to $75 per day, wait three days, then to $100 per day, wait three days, then increase your budget by increments of $50 every three days or so. Even then, the three day period may not be long enough for the algorithm to stabilize again, so if your results go all out of whack, reduce it back down to the previous daily budget and wait a little longer between increments. It's tedious but unfortunately the best way to keep your results on track.

- **Method #2 is "audience scaling"**—to create more ad sets targeting new audiences you haven't tested before. Around 50% of the audiences you test won't get you very good results, but the other half will be viable and can be used to scale how many people see your ads. You should also test the "Lookalike Audience" feature of your customers here, but keep in mind this usually requires an audience size of at least 1,000 people to create an audience that works well for you.

- **Method #3 is "offer scaling"**—to create more offers to advertise to your winning audiences, e.g. lead magnets and front-end products leading people into your proven upsell sequence. This requires the most work, however, and probably won't be needed until you're reaching at least six to seven figures per year in most niches.

There are plenty of other tricks and methods you can use too, but these three are the main ones which always work for me when done correctly.

But what if you don't know *what* to test across your entire business, because you aren't sure what people want? This is when you revisit the research stage and have as many conversations with your potential customers as possible.

Typically, when working with a new client, I'll visit places where their ideal prospects hang out, including Facebook groups closely related to their topic, message boards / forums, and similar. Then I'll ask them to complete a short three question survey asking:

1) Which aspects they want to learn more about.

2) What their biggest problem is right now.

3) If we designed a perfect product to help you, what would you want it to be like?

Of course, nobody will jump out of their shoes to answer a survey, so it's usually best to incentivize them to do so by offering a chance to win a $10 Amazon Gift Card for all completed entries.

If you can, you should also ask them for a follow-up conversation on the phone to delve deeper into their answers, again incentivizing them to do so in some way.

It may seem like an unnecessary expense at this point but understanding what your customers *actually* want—instead of what you *think* they want—is THE most valuable thing you can do in your business, and it is the number one thing stopping you from hitting six or seven figures in the next few months.

As soon as you've revisited what your customers actually want, you just need to edit your marketing to give it to them. Preferably using the exact same language they use, the exact same problems they're experiencing, and the exact same emotions they are going through.

This will hit their "emotional bullseye," so they see you as a perfect fit to help them.

When doing all this testing and extended research, you'll start to see this venture as a *real business* instead of a "side project" or hobby, even if you're working on your laptop in your underwear. This is great, because if you see it as a hobby, you'll earn a hobby income. But if you see it as a business, you'll earn a business income. It's the mindset that matters.

Then because you know your prospects inside and out, your results keep getting better and better, people around you start noticing and asking you what you're doing and how you did it.

In my case, I was able to quit my day job at this point and focus on running and growing this business full-time. The people who were originally doubting me were now asking for advice and congratulating me, they were confused at how I was able to earn more than they do while working from home and without having to endure the dreaded daily commute.

They were shocked when I took a month-long vacation in Italy, then soon after I got back, posted a photo on Facebook of my newly-purchased Maserati Granturismo Sport, as they assumed I was a failure because I didn't have a high-profile job like an accountant, lawyer or something in the banking industry. It was a pretty good feeling!

But there's one thing that really catapulted my success even further, which we'll cover in the next stage of growing your online business...

STAGE 9: PREMIUM OFFERS

At this stage, you'll probably be making anywhere between $1,000 USD to $5,000 USD per month in sales, depending on how well you know your audience and how much optimization you've been doing. Sometimes you'll be making more than that.

However exciting this may seem, this is still a start-up income, and there are two main ways to grow your income further:

1) Acquire a higher *volume* of customers.
2) Increase your average Lifetime Customer Value ("LCV" for short), i.e. how much your customers spend with you in total, across all of their purchases from you.

Now, obviously we want to do both, but it's usually pretty difficult to scale your profit if you only have a small profit margin due to only having low to medium priced offers at this point.

That's why we'll first focus on expanding your product line into more premium offers (sometimes called "high-ticket" offers), then scale from there.

Here's why…

If you have a product line consisting of a $27, $37, $97 and $497 offer, that's a maximum potential of $658 per customer, assuming they buy *everything*, every time.

Of course, that's not going to happen, so your average Lifetime Customer Value across all your customers at this point will probably be in the range of around $100—assuming you've been optimizing your sales pages with various split tests.

Essentially, this means you're able to spend $50 on advertising to acquire a customer if you want to get a 2X ROI, i.e. double your money. Or if you're in the mood for some aggressive split testing, it should take you $25 in advertising to acquire a customer if you want to get a 4X ROI.

But this is a lot harder than it sounds—especially with the rising costs of advertising and other overheads in your business when it grows beyond six figures per year.

However, by attempting this, you're playing the game with your hands tied behind your back.

A much easier way is simply to introduce a premium offer into your product line. By doing this, your average Lifetime Customer Value will jump from $100 to around $250.

This is not some made up number either—it's taken from my own statistics, with around 5% of my $27 customers buying my $3000 coaching program.

This increased average Lifetime Customer Value figure means you can now spend up to $125 in advertising to acquire a new customer and still get a 2X ROI (as you'd spend $125 to make $250). Better yet, if your *Profit Process* is optimized well to the point where you're able to acquire a customer for just $62.50 in ad spend, this would get you a 4X ROI (as you'd spend $62.50 to make $250). Of course, all these numbers are averages across a large enough sample size and will vary depending on how much you've fine-tuned the conversion rates of every step in your *Profit Process*.

That's a pretty big difference from only being able to spend $25, right?

This increased number means you can screw everything up and still find it relatively easy to make a profit on your advertising. It's now like having your hands untied and playing the game on easy mode.

Now, you understand the math behind the profit and you're probably wondering how you can implement one of these premium offers.

Well the customers who have already bought something from you will often keep buying what you put in front of them, assuming the offer is good, you've helped them before, the value is there and it's something that will benefit them in their current situation.

Speaking about their current situation, think about their journey so far...

They purchased your low-priced offer(s) because they wanted to learn how to do something themselves. However, this is a "one size fits all" video course, and inevitably people will get *stuck* at some point along the way, or have *questions* relating to their specific circumstances.

That's why the easiest and most effective premium offer to implement at this stage is a consulting offer.

It requires virtually no upfront work because you're not creating another course or program, and it's the easiest type of premium offer to sell because the value is self-explanatory. They'll be chatting with who *they* see as a celebrity (i.e. you).

But what exactly *is* consulting in this context, specifically?

Consulting is simply speaking with your clients 1-on-1 to answer their questions and guide them in the right direction to achieve their goals.

No stone is left unturned—you tell them everything you can to help them achieve their goals.

This is usually done online via a Skype call, giving them one hour with you per week and direct contact with you via your personal email address to answer any questions between calls.

I'd also recommend recording the calls and uploading them to a secure page members area for them, so they can go back over the things you said in the call if necessary, too.

Because of the personalized service, this obviously comes at a price to both you and the customer. Let me explain…

Back in 2010, my customers were constantly asking me questions and begging me to help them with their businesses on a more personal basis. I kept declining for a long time because I liked the idea of a business where I didn't have to block out time in my schedule and actually speak to people *(shock horror!)*.

But soon enough, I had so many requests that it didn't make any sense to say no anymore, so I started accepting new consulting clients at $1000 per month, per client.

Within two days of announcing the service, I had 10 clients. That was an instant $10,000 per month without any upfront work. I was ecstatic!

Although I was hesitant about whether I was able to help everyone because I didn't have the most confidence in my skills back then, and I wasn't the greatest speaker, I gave it a try anyway. My thought process was that I could always refund the customer if it wasn't working out.

Luckily, I was able to help every one of them, all of my clients made back more than they'd paid for the consulting, and I gave many of the clients who followed my advice their first $1000 days.

Another side-benefit of speaking to people in this way is that you get to know a LOT about your customers—their biggest problems, their biggest desires, what makes them frustrated, where they get stuck in the process, and everything that makes them tick. This is a real goldmine to improve your marketing even further and get better at helping people.

Although, as time went on, I started noticing a few flaws with this method...

First, clients were dropping off the radar and not responding to emails or phone calls—most likely because they didn't do the work I asked them to do—which made me look bad as a coach when other customers asked what results my clients were getting.

Second, my clients who took massive action would feel they were now on the right path and didn't need to pay $1,000 per month any more. Although it was sad for me to no longer work with these clients and I lost the dependable income from them working with me, in all honesty it wasn't really an issue, as new people were always waiting to join when a new slot in the service became available.

But most importantly, I was spending roughly 10 hours per week on 1-on-1 calls, and around another five hours per week replying to emails from clients.

Although that was earning me $10,000 per month for 15 hours of work per week, I realized the only way to increase my income was to take on more clients. So, I took on five more clients, which upped my income to $15,000 per month *solely* from this premium offer, but also upped my workload to around 22-24 hours per week.

Around two years into running this service, I felt like I had a job, as I was tied to my laptop due to all the pre-scheduled

203

calls. Even when I was on vacation, I had to spend a few hours per day just keeping up with the barrage of emails I was receiving from these clients, even though they knew I was on vacation.

It was great money, and many entrepreneurs would be happy to tolerate the increased workload for the bigger paycheck. I certainly did for those two years, and it allowed me to buy my first house—a 4-bedroom converted chapel in the English countryside.

Moving to my dream house was an incredible feeling—especially as my first house. I couldn't believe it was actually happening to me, and not some celebrity I was following on TV or social media.

I *love* houses with character—and this had plenty. The living room was triple-height, with the original beams stretching from one end to the other. The windows were original stained glass. There was even a library on a mezzanine!

Better yet, outside the air was clean, the neighborhood was quiet and there wasn't a skyscraper in sight.

Although this was my dream place to live at the time, I'd lost my freedom to achieve it, which definitely wasn't the reason I first got started with an online business. So, I had to make a change.

That's when I got thinking about ways to automate the consulting process.

After speaking with my consulting clients to see what would work best for them, I came up with a plan that worked better than peanut butter and jelly, and one that I've been using ever since.

The concept is, *after* you've acquired enough experience helping people with the 1-on-1 consulting (otherwise it'll be difficult to know exactly what people *actually* want, instead of what you *think* they want), you should turn the 1-on-1 consulting service into a group coaching program.

But it shouldn't be just a generic coaching program around your topic. Everyone does that, and it does nothing to differentiate your stuff in the marketplace.

Instead, your group coaching program should walk people through a set process to achieve a *specific goal* and charge a one-time price to achieve it. I'd recommend starting at $2000 and increasing it to $3000 after your first 10 clients.

The beauty of this is, because the focus of the coaching program is on achieving a *specific* goal instead of just "becoming better" at a topic, they're essentially trading a smaller monetary amount for a larger one.

Or, if you're not helping them to achieve a monetary goal (e.g. the self-improvement niche), you can find their common goal that is worth more than the price of your coaching program to them and have them achieve that.

After working with the consulting clients for two years, even though they all had their own specific issues and different niches to build a business in, I realized that all of them followed a very similar process. Many of them had the same goal, too— to first reach $5000 in profit per month, then finally reach $10,000 in profit per month. So, reaching $10,000 per month became my focus of the coaching program.

Once that was decided, I created an outline based on the common themes that all my consulting clients had followed. With that outline, I created a step-by-step video course, teaching and demonstrating (live on screen) everything I would typically show a consulting client, as if they were there in the room with me, until they reached the common goal (in this case, $10,000 per month).

But this wasn't a normal video course. I knew people wanted the personalized help at this premium price point, so at the end of each video, I would provide action steps for them to follow before progressing onto the next video.

For example, if one video was showing them how to set up their email list, their action steps would be to set up their email list exactly as I demonstrated in the video. That way they could follow along, as if I was in the room with them.

I'd then add these coaching videos to Vimeo (in the same way as I did for my low-priced products), but then add them into a separate WordPress members area JUST for this premium coaching program, e.g. https://coaching.yourdomain.com . This helps people to feel like you've pulled back the velvet rope to a secret area of your website, increasing the perceived value you're providing to them.

Also, I would always tell them to ask me as many questions as they liked within the dedicated Facebook group—just for the students of the coaching program. In there, I would answer their questions every day.

At first, I wasn't sure if people would find that compelling, but it turns out people love the sense of community that comes with a group experience. Many business partnerships and friendships have been made since then, and most people actually *prefer* going through the process with other people instead of the often-isolating experience that 1-on-1 coaching brings.

In addition to the Facebook group, I wanted to ensure people still had the "live" experience of chatting with me, so I added the final element to the coaching program—live weekly calls with me and the rest of the group.

Note here that this is not a 1-on-1 coaching call for every client, but instead *one* weekly live call where all of the students get on the call at the same time.

I would teach something new, re-iterate important points or share "what's working now" for the first 20-30 minutes of the call, then open it up for questions. The questions could be submitted in the Facebook group before the call, or in the chat box live on the call.

This was pretty easy to do, as I would use GoToWebinar to set a recurring weekly webinar at the same date and time, and I've done so ever since. This way, people have just one link to use for every weekly session.

So, to recap, this particular type of the coaching program should include:

1) A step-by-step program/course to follow that provides them with the overall "curriculum," having each video ending with action steps and a quick mention to *please* ask any questions within the private Facebook group (so they still feel that sense of 1-on-1 interaction with you). This should ideally be housed within a separate WordPress members area to keep it separate to your lower-priced entry-level products, such as https://coaching.yourdomain.com.

2) An area for them to ask you questions—a private Facebook group. Note that this should be a "Secret" group (invisible to outsiders) instead of a "Closed" group, so other marketers can't poach your valuable clients.

3) A weekly live coaching webinar/call where your clients learn something new and have the ability to ask you questions live on air. I personally recommend they type out their questions in the chat box rather than unmuting people to speak via their microphone, as we trialed it once and found that either people couldn't figure out how to get their microphone to work properly, or they tend to dance around the question for a while talking about their dog and two kids live on air—but either way it becomes awkward for everyone involved. We also look after for the clients who can't attend live (due to their day job or other life commitments) by providing the recording for every weekly live session in the members area, within two hours of the call ending.

Using this process, I was able to cut my workload down from around 22-24 hours per week for 15 clients, to around four hours per week serving 250+ clients, each having paid upwards of $3,000 for this one service alone.

Yep—4 hours per week for 250+ coaching clients. This was made possible because not everyone asks questions in the Facebook group, and not everyone attends the live sessions. When they first join, they usually ask a ton of questions for the first month or so, then quiet down once they fully understand the path they need to follow.

So, out of those 250+ clients, only around 20 of them are regularly asking questions every week, many of which are fairly easy to answer.

This is pretty crazy (and disappointing from my point of view) considering they paid $3,000 to join; however, you can lead a horse to water, but you can't make it drink.

In terms of profit, here's how that works out:

- **Before:** 15 clients X $1,000 per month = $15,000 per month. Realistically most people would drop off after around 5-6 months after they got the help they needed, so that's **$90,000 per year in the best case scenario**, while working my ass off, feeling exhausted all the time and not having the freedom I was used to.

- **After:** 250+ clients X $3,000 one time = **$750,000+**, while having SO much more free time, happier clients due to the community feeling and not working too hard.

But it wasn't all good…

By the time I'd restructured this coaching program into a group program and gained all those clients to make more money while working less, it was too late. My wife had already asked for a divorce due to me focusing too much on work and not making enough time for her and the family, amongst many other reasons.

This did allow me to gain a new lease on life by moving to a rented apartment in London to enjoy the vivacious city life I'd never had before. I loved it! The new place wasn't quite a chapel, but instead a remodeled hospital converted into luxury apartments. I guess I just can't live in a normal house!

So, don't fall into the same relationship-destroying trap like I did, working too much because of relying on 1-on-1 clients, always trading time for dollars. I guess I had to make that mistake so you don't have to. I'm glad I did, but you can never get that time back.

Now in hindsight, charging one set price for lifetime access to the group coaching program was both a good idea and a bad idea. It was a good idea because it separated me from everyone else in the marketplace, but also a bad idea because it didn't provide any way to generate more revenue from those enrolled coaching clients at the time. So, I wish I would have tested having a set time limit on the coaching elements—maybe a year of access to me, then a further $1000 per year to keep access to the coaching group and live weekly calls. However, I feel the one-time price is what made it compelling to a lot of my clients, compared to my competitors who are charging monthly or yearly. It's just another way to go above and beyond what everyone else is doing.

But once you have this program structured, created and set up, what is the best way to enroll clients into it?

With low-priced offers, it's super effective to show people a sales page explaining what the product is and why they should buy it. But that won't work with high-priced offers due to there being more risk involved for the prospect.

So instead, you need to have a more personalized sales process. Here's what it looks like:

This same process is what turns roughly 5% of my $27 purchasers into $3000 coaching clients. Here's the process in more detail…

First, you need to deliver some valuable content related to the topic of your coaching program.

A webinar works really well here, as you can present it live once and then automate it using solutions like EverWebinar, allowing you to keep it running all the time and get new clients 24/7/365, anywhere in the world. But if you're not comfortable presenting live, alternatively a 20-30 minute video gets around half the results of a webinar.

Ideally what you teach in this free content should be either:

a) An *overview* of the steps they need to take to achieve the *same* end goal as your coaching program helps them to achieve, or...

b) An in-depth lesson about *one* of the topics covered in the coaching program.

So, for example, my coaching program helps people to make $10k per month online, meaning my free webinar teaches people "The 7 Steps To Make $10k Per Month Online."

If your coaching program helps people to lose 30 pounds, your webinar could be about "The 5 Steps To Shed 30 Pounds Without Feeling Hungry All Day Or Killing Yourself In The Gym," OR about the best exercises to reduce your body fat percentage. You get the idea.

At the end of this free content, you should briefly introduce your coaching program and what it helps people to achieve, then ask them to submit a short online application form if they want to learn more about it and see if it's right for them. Explain that the application process is in place because you only work with action takers and you're very selective with who you work with (which should be true anyway).

Note here how we're not giving them the price along with an opportunity to buy the program within the content itself— but instead *only* giving them the basics about it and asking them to apply for it, due to it being extremely limited. This is for one simple reason... If you look at the high-priced offers in everyday life, they are usually either rare, valuable or both. We're manufacturing that same feeling here by hiding our offer behind the "velvet rope," i.e. the application form.

Plus, people need to understand the value of the program and how it relates to their specific situation before knowing the price too, otherwise the price isn't justified, and it creates a knee-jerk reaction that it's "too expensive." So, don't mention the price, but you can say "it's not cheap" or some variation of that to discourage the people who won't be able to afford it.

The application form itself has a few important questions about themselves, all of which are open-ended text fields for them to write their answer:

- Your name
- Phone number
- Email
- When Is The Best Time To Call You? (Please Include Your Time Zone)
- Country
- What is your CURRENT _____? (Note: Fill in the blank in this question with something to let you know how well they're getting along with the topic of your niche, e.g. "monthly income from your online business," "weight," "happiness with your dog's behavior," etc.)
- What is your TARGET _____? (Note: Same principle as above.)
- Please be completely honest... Why haven't you hit your target yet?
- What most influenced your decision to complete this application today and reach out to me?
- How WILLING and ABLE are you to invest in achieving your goals? (time, finances, resources, current commitments, etc.)
- Is there anything else I should know when considering your application?

... Then after a while, we added this question:

☐ Complete this sentence: James, when working on my business I am a...

... With three multiple choice answers as follows:

a) "Excuse maker" who seeks out opportunities but then finds convenient "reasons" not to take advantage of them.

b) "Procrastinator" who decided YES but then doesn't pull the trigger until the opportunity has passed.

c) "Action-Taker" who sees the opportunity, grabs it with both hands, and moves forward fast.

... Which helped people to reconfirm in their mind that they were indeed an action-taker, and action-takers take advantage of opportunities (i.e. buying your coaching program).

Plus, we found that a lot of people weren't picking up the phone, so we added this question:

"Finally, please confirm you will actually pick up the phone to chat with my friendly assistant Leigh about your application:"

... With the one checkbox answer as:

☐ Yes James, I WILL pick up the phone when I see a phone number I don't recognize. I understand that if I miss this call, I will forfeit my opportunity.

... Which drastically increased the number of people who actually picked up the phone when we called them, due to the "fear of loss" from missing out on their opportunity.

Note: If you don't have an assistant yet, just change the wording in the question accordingly. Also remember to change "James" to your own name, if your name isn't James.

But how do you get people to see the free content and/or submit an application form?

The good news is, we can "bolt on" this offer to what you already have. Using what I'm about to explain to you, we're able to convert above 5% of customers who purchase our $27 product into spending $3,000 or more with us—yet nobody is doing this stuff!

First, you can simply add a vertical "Need Some Help?" graphic to the right side of every page of your members area. When clicked, it takes them to a page with a short video explaining that you've had some requests from other customers for some additional hand-holding. That's where you refer them to your high-ticket offer, preferably a coaching program or something with a 4- or 5-figure price tag to make the most of the opportunity and provide the most value possible to your customers.

Next, you should have a "bonus training" for customers only, made obvious within the first page of the members area so people can't miss it. This sends people to your free content discussed above, giving them value related to the program and ending with a soft sell for your primary high-ticket offer. Personally, we use EverWebinar to set this up, but as long as the outcome is the same, it doesn't matter which solution you use to achieve it.

After that, I usually wait seven days after they've joined our front-end product, then put them into an email follow-up sequence, promoting the same bonus training webinar (as mentioned above) in case they missed it. Whether they attend or not, I usually promote a different "simulated live" training for free, again ending with a promotion for your high-ticket offer.

If you want to really ramp this up, you could also show retargeting ads on Facebook, Google and elsewhere to remind them to register for and attend the bonus training(s).

Doing all of these things *without* any marketing to your existing subscribers and customers via your email list, you should get around 3-4 applications per week at the very minimum if you're acquiring a decent number of customers from your front-end product.

When the applications come in, you should give them a call at the time they specified on the form, as soon as possible.

Around half of the people will say it's not a good time for them, so just reschedule at a time that works best for them. Then the other half will usually have no issues having the call right there and then. In this case, simply speak to them on the phone for roughly 30-45 minutes in a friendly, conversational, no-pressure way about:

1) Where they are right now (i.e. their struggles, pain points, why they need to move forward now, etc.).

2) Where they want to be (i.e. their goals, desires, why it's important to them, etc.).

3) If your premium program can help them bridge the gap between where they are right now and where they want to be, in their own words.

It's super important to do all of this in a way that's friendly, conversational and without any selling pressure, otherwise you're going to push them away—and at that point, you've just lost a client.

In other words, you shouldn't be talking much on this call at all. They should do 80% of the talking by answering your questions, as you dig deeper and deeper into what they're telling you in each stage of the call. Be as specific as possible!

For example, if they say they want to make $10,000 per month with an online business, ask them why! What would they spend that money on, specifically? How would it make them feel? Where would they go on vacation, specifically?

The more specific they can be with their answers, the easier it will be to get them to say "yes" to joining your coaching program at the end, because they'll see the value and transformation you're providing to them.

If at the end of the call they're happy with the full details of the program and are ready to move forward, simply email them the link to the order form and stay on the phone while they complete it and pay, "just to help if anything goes wrong."

If you hang up the phone and give them the link, it takes them out of the buying state you just spent 30-40 minutes developing with them, and they'll suddenly get nervous about taking the leap of faith, meaning the chance of them buying is drastically reduced. So be sure to stay on the phone until their payment has gone through—even if it does feel a little awkward to sit there in silence, being very aware of how loud you're breathing while they do it.

Sometimes you'll speak to people who genuinely *are* action takers, but they simply can't afford the $3,000 in one payment, right there on the phone. In this case, feel free to offer them a payment plan where you split up the fee into equal monthly payments—but keep in mind that not everyone will complete these payments and it's a lot of hassle to chase these people down, so a full payment is preferred.

There are options like paying with PayPal Credit, meaning you get the full amount up front instead of waiting for their monthly payments to come through—but this is usually hit and miss depending on where in the world the prospect is located.

On the other side of the coin, sometimes you'll speak to people who say they "can't afford it" (even when offered a payment plan), or some other excuse for not moving forward. These reasons for not buying (called "objections" in the selling world) are all symptoms of you **not demonstrating your value to the client well enough**.

To give you an example, if you tried selling them a lottery ticket for $20,000, they'd probably say that's "too expensive," "they can't afford it," and/or "you're crazy." But then if you explained it was the winning ticket from last night's draw for the guaranteed jackpot of $20 million dollars, you can bet they'd jump out of their chair and do anything they could to find that money before somebody else bought it, even if they didn't have the money to begin with.

So, it all comes down to the value—and the transformation—you're presenting to them.

Ideally you should be enrolling at least 20% of the people you speak to on the phone. If you're enrolling any less than that, there's something seriously wrong with either your conversation with them or your offer's hook in general. Maybe you're trying to sell too hard, and/or maybe people don't want the goal you're promising them. So, try changing one or the other.

But if you're enrolling around 20% of the people you speak to, there's room for improvement in your conversation and the questions you're asking them. Try digging deeper into the pain they're explaining to you and get more specific with everything.

If you're doing the calls yourself, it should be pretty easy to close people, so your closing rate will usually be above 50% if you're running the conversation correctly. However, if you have an assistant doing the calls for you, anything above 30% is great and you should be pleased.

On that topic, it's usually best to start off doing the calls yourself, then use your experiences to write a loose script to follow in the conversation. Find out what works well, what doesn't work, and edit the script accordingly. Then, once you've got the process down pretty consistently, you can hire someone else and pass the loose script to them, freeing up your time once again.

I say "loose script" because it shouldn't be word-for-word, otherwise it's going to sound robotic and... scripted. Instead, just have a few bullets reminding you of which questions to ask and to keep the conversation flowing in the direction you want it to.

After that, it's just a matter of looking after the client as much as possible and delivering on your promises as a coach.

This same selling process works amazingly well to sell anything priced above $1000, without feeling like a high-pressure used car salesperson.

In fact, after selling my $3000 coaching program in this way for a long time, I also sold a very premium offer for $20,000 using the exact same process, and it sells out every time I open it up—currently to a total of 20 clients. I also know other B2B business owners using this same strategy to sell packages for upwards of $100,000 per client. People always want to buy more!

If people have enough pain to escape their current situation and enough desire to achieve their goals, they'll pay whatever it takes. Don't get in your own head about the high prices—let the market tell you what they can and can't afford. You'll be surprised. Just like I was when I first started charging higher prices...

When I transitioned from the $1,000 per month consulting service into the $3,000 upfront one-time group coaching program, the first thought in my head was, "why would somebody pay me $3000? I'm not an expert."

These doubts are completely normal, but the only way to overcome them is to put yourself in the mind of your prospect. If they're suffering with a problem every day of their life, always there at the back of their mind, it takes its toll on them. When that inner pain becomes severe enough, they'll often do anything to escape it and achieve their goals. It may take some people longer than others, but it happens to us all eventually.

Not only that, but even if you don't think of yourself as an expert, it's all down to how other people *perceive* you. If you're there on camera in a video course, or teaching them something in a book, they *perceive* you to be in a position of authority—and therefore an expert *compared to them*. It's all relative.

When I realized this, I thought, What the heck, let's try it and see how it works.

It just so happens that thought went on to generate over $750,000 in coaching sales, and I wouldn't have been able to make that money—or help all those people around the world—without taking that initial leap of faith.

So, don't let your own doubts and false beliefs get in your own way of success, or helping people who need to be helped. After all, who are you to deny them a solution?

Once you overcome this mental block, implement a premium solution like this and market it correctly, it's quite common for your profit to double or even triple almost overnight due to the way the math works out.

It would take you 112 customers buying a $27 product to make $3000—most of which is swallowed by advertising costs—yet it only takes *one* customer to buy your coaching program to make the same amount in pure profit (as the advertising costs to acquire the customer have already been paid by then).

And I can tell you with 100% certainty, it's much easier to make one sale of a premium offer to an existing customer than acquire 112 brand new customers from scratch.

This stage of your business is really where your perfect lifestyle *really* becomes a reality. You're often able to easily quit your day job and work on your business full time, then your daily life will usually consist of answering a few questions in your coaching group, replying to emails from people interested in your coaching program, working on new content, and maintaining what you've built until now.

You're making more money than you've most likely ever experienced before, and people start noticing. Especially when you use some of that money to buy a Lamborghini Huracan (with a race exhaust) like I did. Logically it was a terrible financial decision, but emotionally it was the best thing I've ever done, as I'm a giant car fanatic and it's been my dream since day one. It only felt natural to capture the collection of that dream on camera, so it's visible on my blog if you're interested.

Personally, I always try to live my personal life based on emotion, and my business life based on logic, and I find that works pretty well for me.

But as an entrepreneur, after following this routine for a while, it sometimes becomes a little too mundane and it's easy to start looking for ways to grow your legacy even further. So, here's how to do just that...

STAGE 10: SCALING

When I first started making above $10,000 per month in profit, life was good.

I was comparing myself to people around me, and in all honesty, I was leagues ahead. I didn't look at prices when shopping for food any more, as I was earning more in one or two months than most people earned in a year. I also started to get a little bit of an ego.

But when you're at this stage, you'll often start to network with people who are doing even better than you, which quickly knocks your ego back down to earth. In my case, this was joining a supercar owners club, filled with people making over $50,000 per month, $100,000 per month, and even $1MM+ per month. Suddenly, your 6-figure income doesn't seem so great. Then you want more!

But you realize there are a few things stopping you from achieving that same high 6-figure—or 7-figure—income.

The first is the lack of *time* available in the day to get everything done. If you've found yourself working later than you'd planned and/or saying, "If only there were more hours in the day, I could...", then that's a major symptom of this problem.

The second bottleneck is the lack of *expertise*. If you've found yourself creating sub-par graphics, website pages, videos or anything else where you feel it's "only just good enough"— which inevitably limits the results you're getting—then this one is for you. Procrastinating items on your to-do list also falls under this category, as that's a symptom of not being truly excited or passionate about that particular topic.

Both can be solved by focusing on your core competencies and find another way to get the other stuff done. You aren't good at everything and you don't have to be. Plus, if you try to do everything yourself without any help, you're forever going to get the results you've always gotten.

So, to fix this, list all your business's tasks in three categories:

1) What are you good at?
2) What do *you personally* NEED to do? (i.e. realistically, nobody else can do this but you.)
3) Which tasks are left over?

Here's a quick one for me:

Category #1: What am I good at?	Category #2: What do I *personally* NEED to do?	Category #3: Which tasks are left over?
1) Content creation 2) Advertising 3) Enrolling clients on the phone. 4) Creating good marketing angles/hooks. 5) ~~Stroking cats.~~	1) Content creation (but realistically that can be outsourced too) 2) Reply to personal emails.	1) Graphic design 2) Web page design 3) Customer support 4) SEO 5) Writing sales copy. 6) Video creation (recording, editing, etc.).

Then your first focus is to find somebody else to do the tasks in category #3, as these are the current bottlenecks stopping you from growing your business's income.

You can also have someone else take over the tasks in category #1 that *aren't* in category #2 (e.g. advertising in the above example), but this is really just to free up more time in your daily schedule.

Now, "hiring people" doesn't always necessarily mean renting out office space and filling it up with employees. Personally, this idea never appealed to me, as it would mean getting out of bed before 9 am every day and having to deal with extra stresses in my daily life, which are the exact things I created this online business to avoid—not to mention the additional costly overheads that come with managing people in an office environment. So, instead, I prefer to hire and manage my employees online. There are two ways you can do this…

The first way is to hire a freelancer and create a good relationship with them in the long-term, so they're able to work on your tasks and get them done quickly for a reasonable price. This is usually the best option to start with, as you won't know how much work you'll have for them until they actually start, and it wouldn't make sense to pay someone for 40 hours per week if they only have five hours of work to do per week. So therefore, hiring a freelancer is usually a better option for inconsistent workloads or to be used as and when you need them.

I've found UpWork.com to be a great place to hire people, as it allows you to see people's previous work and their reviews from previous employers, so you know they live up to their promises. Simply post a job with as much detail in the job description as possible, then weed out the amateurs based on the reviews from their previous work.

Don't hire the cheapest candidate(s), as these are often cheap for a reason. Hire cheap, hire twice.

Instead, you should focus on hiring people who speak the same language as you (it goes without saying, but you'd be surprised by the people some of my clients have hired in the past), have experience with exactly the same tasks you're looking to hire out, and have at least a four star rating.

It may be difficult to narrow down to one candidate if you have a good application pool, so in this scenario I'll usually give all of them a small paid task to do. Depending on how cruel you're feeling, you can make this easy or hard to accomplish, but the harder tasks will usually make the best candidate rise to the top. Just be sure this *is* a small task and the pay is adequate for what you're asking of them, otherwise you can offend some people as they'll think you're taking advantage of them.

I've hired a video editor, a Conversion Rate Optimization (CRO) expert, a programmer and an SEO expert this way, and they're still working for me to this day, as and when I need them.

The second way is to hire somebody "in house," i.e. they are primarily focused on working with your company and are classed as your "employee."

Typically, I'll do this once I've had some experience with a freelancer, *or* when the task needs a large chunk of time per week. A good example of this is a customer service manager. To begin with, I was replying to all my customer service tickets and emails myself, which was not only very time-consuming (usually taking around 2-3 hours per day out of my schedule), but also not the best use of my time, nor good for my branding and positioning.

So, when a great customer service manager got in touch with me (making things easy!), I jumped at the chance to hire him, and he's been with us ever since. Now, I personally read all my customer support tickets and emails to keep on the same level as my prospects and customers (taking around 15 minutes per day), but my customer support manager replies to them. And I'm sure I'll be hiring other customer support representatives in the future when he gets overworked, too.

However, you may not be lucky enough to have someone with great skills approach you, so you'll most likely have to either:

a) Use UpWork.com or Freelancer.com to hire a freelancer to begin with, then after they've been doing good work for a while, ask if they want to work exclusively for you on a set monthly contract.

b) Place a job listing on Craigslist (yes, I've seen it work before!) or another popular hiring website in your country (e.g. Indeed.com, Monster.com, LinkedIn.com, etc.).

c) Send an email to your email list, explaining the available position, what it entails and how to get in touch with you about it.

I usually start with option (c), as the people on your newsletter will most likely already know a lot about your business and the information it teaches, so the training process will become much easier. After that, I'll usually go to option (a).

Then it's just a matter of doing the usual sifting and sorting process, speaking to the best candidates and setting up informal interviews with them on Skype or similar. Just be sure you've chosen the right candidate, as making the wrong hire can be a real pain in the backside.

I once hired what seemed like a competent, polite lady to speak to our coaching program applicants, following a very loose script as explained earlier in this book. In our interview, she spoke clearly and really impressed me with what she had to say. But when it came to actually speak to our coaching program applicants, after listening to the recordings of her phone calls, she suddenly got really nervous and sounded like she was making a 911 call. Needless to say, the clients didn't buy, and we had to hire someone else, but we probably lost about 4-5 new coaching clients—$12,000 to $15,000—because of that bad hire.

You can't *always* avoid bad hires though—it's just a matter of doing the best you can with the experience you have. Hire slow and fire fast (usually after three "oh, come on!" moments).

Once you've found someone, training them can take a while depending on the task they'll be doing and their level of experience. I usually take people on who have a medium level of experience and skills, so their pay rate isn't at the executive level, but I can still train them to reach our expected high standards.

As they already have some experience, it's often pretty easy for people to get settled in and learn the ropes. We usually do any kind of teaching within a GoToMeeting room or Skype call, making sure to record the sessions so they can look back on them in future if necessary.

If you find yourself needing to hire a LOT of people for the same role—for example, a customer support representative or a salesperson to enroll your coaching clients—it's often a giant timesaver to record a video course with what you'd teach them

1-on-1 and give *that* to them instead. After they've consumed the material, give them a quiz to double-check what they've learned and ask if they have any questions before starting.

They should be 100% clear on what's expected of them before starting the role—not "learning as they go along"—as you want to minimize any bad customer experiences which could negatively impact your business.

For example, I was once in a bar with my friends for New Year's Eve, and a *newly-hired* waiter there said we could have a bottle of champagne for free because we bought so many drinks and places at two of their tables. We were thrilled, so we celebrated with the champagne and enjoyed our night. About two hours later, the manager came to our table and said we had to *pay* for the bottle of champagne right now because the first newly-hired waiter had made a mistake—but the truth is, we wouldn't have agreed to the champagne if we'd have known it wasn't free, as we already had too many drinks to go around. Needless to say, we won't be going back there again. One small mistake from a new hire, one huge negative impact on a potential long-term customer who spends way more than he should on nights out with friends. This experience did have a positive impact on me too though, as we now *always* make sure to live up to all our promises, so my customers don't have to experience the same disappointment.

But all hires aren't created equal. You should hire people for some roles before others, as these "high value" roles will have the biggest impact on your business's bottom line.

Namely, these are the roles you should hire for first, depending on how urgent they are to you when you're at this stage of your business's growth:

1) **Customer service manager**—Answers all customer support tickets, emails and social media messages/posts asking you questions. This is often born out of necessity, but they will often persuade prospects sitting on the fence to buy your products and services just by answering a few simple questions. So, they often pay for themselves AND maintain your good relationships with your audience.

2) **Salesperson**—Organizes and conducts the enrollment calls for your premium offers. I say "salesperson" lightly, as they're more of a "conversation facilitator" rather than somebody who sells through pressure.

3) **Copywriter**—If your sales pages don't convert well, your business isn't going to stay around for very long. So, a copywriter is a necessity if you don't have several years to learn how to write persuasive sales page copy for your paid offers. They usually charge a flat fee for each sales page or sales video script you'd like written, and they aren't cheap—but the results always pay for the initial fee multiple times over. For example, the sales page copy for my $27 offer cost me $3,000 to get written, but so far that exact copy has allowed me to make over $1.6MM in sales. So, you'll get a pretty good ROI if you choose the right person.

4) **Graphics Designer**—Another way to bump up your conversion rates is to make your sales pages more visually appealing. Getting a freelance graphic designer to spruce up our sales pages is now standard procedure for every new offer we create, because it *always* increases our conversion rate by a considerable amount (sometimes *double* what it was before). I repeat, *not*

once has it made things worse. Again, a wise investment if you hire the right person.

Now, of course these hires aren't free. You need to find the money out of your profits to pay for them. Not to mention there are plenty of other costs at this stage of your business with new tools, new advertising possibilities, and more.

I'll always remember the scene in the movie *Limitless*, where the main character has discovered a pill that makes him much smarter while he's on it and uses it to bank big on the stock exchange. But using money to make money is all about what you have to start with. So, he finds a way to increase the initial investment to make the multiplied investment much higher. Smart move.

Now, in the movie, the character gets his money from a shady loan shark. That would be a terrible move for you, and I wouldn't suggest that. But instead, there are plenty of other ways to raise capital without losing your shirt.

Before I go on, you should know that nobody else talks about this stuff, because I feel they don't like being put at risk or being held responsible. So, just be sure that if you are going to follow this advice, you always do it *sensibly* and don't ever, ever take any uncalculated risks—especially those based on emotional thinking. Plus, you agree to not hold me responsible for anything negative that happens. You *can* thank me for the positive results if you want to, though.

What most people do is start to look for investors, but personally I'm not a fan of giving away large chunks of my business when I can find the money and expertise elsewhere, while keeping 100% of the business for myself.

So, the first way to raise capital for your business is to use credit cards specifically created for businesses. These often start with a low, manageable line of credit and increase with your spending over time. My personal favorite is the American Express Business Gold Card, as you get reward points for everything you spend. Just by putting my advertising spend on here, I was able to get free flights from the UK to Mexico within a few months. It's a charge card though, so just be sure you keep an eye on your spending and pay it off in full every month.

Although getting a few extra thousand dollars will help, it's not going to drastically change what you can do in your business. That's where the bigger opportunities come into play.

In our business, all of our sales come through our PayPal merchant account, which gives us access to a feature called PayPal Working Capital. It's essentially a low-interest cash advance for your business, calculated based on your sales volume and amount. The more sales you have per month, the higher your allowable cash advance can be. I've used this service to acquire $20,000 in funding without having to give away parts of my business to investors or anyone else, which later turned into over $100,000 in sales. After that first advance was paid off, I used it to acquire $60,000 in funding, which later turned into over $300,000 in sales. I'll show you how later in this chapter.

However, this service has a lot of restrictions based on your location in the world, how much of your business's profit goes through PayPal, and your PayPal account's standing. If you have your account limited (or "banned" temporarily) for policy violations, you can usually kiss this feature goodbye for 2-3 years (yes, that long!). So, this may or may not apply to you, but definitely worth looking into.

Another option is using crowdfunding websites such as CapitalOnTap.com, FundingCircle.com, Iwoca.co.uk and similar. These are all services I used in the UK and therefore may not be available in the USA or elsewhere, but worth looking into. However, Funding Circle definitely accepts applications from the USA and is probably the best place to start out of them all.

Simply complete an application form stating what you'll use the money for, and their team of investors will loan you money over the agreed amount of time, in exchange for receiving the interest payment from the loan. The investors get a higher interest rate than having their money sit in a bank account somewhere, and the business owners are able to use the new funds to grow their business. It's a win/win.

When you get this new funding one way or another, it's firstly exciting, but then it dawns on you... "What specifically should I use this money on?" In my experience, it should be spent on things that speed up your scaling or allow you to multiply profit more effectively.

But here's how *we* used the funding to transform our business from making around $10,000-$20,000 per month to consistently over $70,000 per month, in this order:

1) **Purchased an advertising coaching program**— Although we were using Facebook Ads profitably, I felt it wasn't consistent and our results would always vary from week to week. We also found that our campaigns would saturate quickly, meaning we were always having to come up with new advertising copy, images, and so on. So, we purchased a premium-level Facebook Ads course from Jason Hornung and Justin Brooke, two traffic titans in the online marketing world. We learned SO much we didn't know before, and we felt like we truly mastered the Facebook Ads network, allowing us to create more effective ads and ultimately get a larger return on our ad spend than we were getting before.

2) **Purchased new video equipment**—Previously, I was shooting our videos on a Canon 50D DSLR camera. Not terrible, but the lack of other video equipment to go with it made our videos look less than ideal. The audio wasn't great, the lighting was poor, and they looked like they were recorded in my grandma's basement. So, I bought a few professional lights, a more sturdy camera tripod, a new microphone for recording videos on my laptop (RODE NT-USB), a new shotgun microphone for recording videos to the DSLR camera (Sennheiser MK600), a sturdy stand for both new microphones, a green screen, an autocue (just one to be used with an autocue app on my iPhone), Adobe Premiere Pro, and a few other small purchases. Although this didn't exactly come to thousands of dollars, I was hesitant to purchase them before because I felt I could use our existing budget better elsewhere, like on ads. So, gaining the new capital helped me to overcome that mental barrier and finally take the leap. Now, we had a way to look more professional on video, increasing the authority status and credibility we had with our audience, instead of looking like a part-time operation where I could flee the country at any minute.

3) **Hired a conversion rate optimization (CRO) expert**—We analyzed our business for the biggest opportunities and discovered that although we were doing well with split testing, the most important parts of the funnel, we could be doing better with our analytics for *every* step in our sales funnel. After all, every step has an impact on the next step. So, we hired a full-time CRO expert to set up our analytics properly, so we had the full picture of what was going on with our funnels. He also created visual flowcharts of all our funnels,

including visitor and conversion rate data for the last 30 days (updated automatically every day), allowing us to see which steps of the funnel were leaking results. Ultimately, this led to an extra bump in conversion rates across the board for all of our funnels, getting us a larger ROI from our traffic.

4) **Hired a graphics designer**—Although our sales pages were converting pretty well, they still looked a little bland, and I wasn't really in a hurry to show them off to new prospects. So, we hired a direct-response graphics designer on a freelance "as and when" basis to spruce up all of our pages. We started with the entry-level front-end offer, which increased our conversion rate from 4% to 6%. After that, we had him do the same for the upsell pages, resulting in another noticeable lift in their conversion rates. Then we did the same for the premium offer sales pages and application form pages— which not only increased our application form submissions, but also increased the *quality* of people who were applying, meaning we had a lot more clients we enjoyed working with.

5) **Increased our advertising budget**—Usually you have to wait 30+ days for an advertising campaign to make you a profit, then you re-invest that profit back into more ads, and so on. However, this process has a super long lead time and it can take a while to receive the budget you need to scale up. So, we injected some of the funds we acquired into our ad campaigns, and our ads previously turning $100 in ad spend per day into $300 in sales per day (after the lifetime of the ad campaign) are now turning $500 in ad spend per day into around $1600 in sales per day in a much shorter timeframe, also

due to our new advertising skills and increased conversion rates in our sales funnels.

Notice here how *none* of these purchases were new "cash siphons" or "loopholes." Anything advertised as such is just another way to take your money and isn't a long-term strategy for a successful business.

Plus, none of the purchases were for different business models, because as soon as you go into a different business model, you're not only having to start again from scratch, but you're also dividing your time and resources between two things, instead of focusing everything on one thing. So, always stick to one thing until you've hit your big "bucket list" type goals, and only then should you start working on something else too, if you want to.

Ultimately, the key here is to invest the money wisely in long-term assets for your company, and preferably something that is going to directly generate an increase in your profits. When done right, you can make back the money you've acquired in profit pretty quickly, then pay back the funds early, minimizing the amount of interest you pay.

This is where you go from a one-person start-up into a fully-fledged business. Everything you do is now about getting a positive ROI or having some kind of impact on sales. You reinvest some of your profits back into the business to grow it further, and so on.

By doing this, you'll also start to attract attention—not all of it good. Some people will always offer to "help" you and make bold promises, but few will actually deliver on their promises.

Case in point: At this stage of my business, I thought it would be a great idea to have somebody run my Facebook Ads campaigns for me. After all, this particular agency (no names mentioned) was always showcasing their incredible results from their other high-profile clients and said they could do the same for me—despite having a high-risk business model when it comes to Facebook Ads due to their entry-level employees wrongly interpreting my stuff as "get rich quick" or "MLM" topics, which are against their advertising policies. But they said they'd be fine with it.

At first, I had my doubts, but they assured me they knew what they were doing and set me some pretty positive expectations. So, I hired them with a 3-month contract, at $3,000 per month plus around $3,000 per month in ad spend.

While working with them, I kept my own campaigns running at a massively reduced daily budget so I could compare the "before and after" results of their new campaigns versus mine, in the hope of giving them a positive testimonial afterwards.

Turns out that after three months of trying, they made a NET *loss* of £8,711.17 GBP (around $11,100 USD), while my campaigns made a net profit of £6,040 GBP (around $7,700 USD).

So, what was the expensive lesson learned here? At this stage, you know your business better than anyone. Any doubts that creep into your mind or bad gut feelings you get are just your past, present and future consciousness raising a big red flag for you. In fact, scientists have said this "gut feeling" is your subconscious mind coming to a conclusion based on all the available—and unavailable—knowledge you have at that time. So, listen to it!

I didn't just lose around $11,100 by not listening to my gut, but I also lost three months of opportunities to grow my business myself, or with someone else who could actually deliver on their promises.

So, after that, I decided to start running Facebook Ads for my clients to avoid them having to suffer the same fate. It's quite an origin story.

And to me, that's what is the most valuable. Everything that happens in your business is either a learning experience for the future, or an immediate leap forward for your progress—and sometimes both.

But this self-awareness typically only starts to happen at this stage of your business, as you've had enough *experience* and acquired enough *knowledge* to raise both your marketing IQ and business IQ to a level which makes running and growing your online business effortless.

Just think…

You've acquired years of knowledge and experience and achieved in a few years what most people can only dream of in their entire lifetime.

Not only that, but you'll now have a valuable asset—an online business that generates a profit for you whether you're working or not. A business that allows you to work whenever you want, wherever you want.

Such as right now, I'm writing this book after moving with my girlfriend from London to Mexico City for a change of scenery. The world is our oyster, and it can be yours too.

But you only have your hard work, dedication and perseverance to thank for this.

Your advertisements are now being shown 24/7 to people all over the world who need help. If everything is done correctly, your ideal prospects see these ads and buy your products without hesitation. Your automated systems ensure these new customers have a *great* experience with you and change their lives for the better. Because of the great experience they've had with you, your customers buy *more* of your products and become loyal fans. After all, it's always a win/win for everyone involved.

We now come full circle, as the life I described in the very first chapter becomes a reality. Your daily life involves helping your coaching clients, creating new content at least once per week to generate a natural desire to work with you, and creating new products to cover topics your loyal customers are begging you to help them with. Oh, and not to mention checking your sales stats and feeling so happy to have reached this point.

You will have the occasional battle to fight, but that's just life's way of determining if you're *worthy* of what you've achieved. So, show it who's boss, hold on to what's rightfully yours, and keep moving forward to improve more people's lives all over the world.

Keep growing, keep learning, keep fighting. You are *unstoppable*.

BONUS CHAPTER: THE MOST IMPORTANT LESSONS I'VE LEARNED

Building a business is a wild ride.

Sometimes you'll feel like you're on top of the world when you're making a huge profit—especially when you make your first low-ticket, medium-ticket and high-ticket sales...

... And other times you'll feel like the whole world is crumbling around you.

But it's the people who persevere through these hard times that are rewarded with a life-changing business that they're pleased to wake up to every morning.

I remember one specific hard time a few years ago when I was in a car crash, I had a period of anxiety attacks, my wife at the time had a brain tumor scare, my mother-in-law at the time died twice but was resuscitated both times, another family member attempted suicide, I had a giant tax bill from the government, which was larger than I expected and struggled to pay off on time, we'd adopted a dog who had a whole host of behavior issues, and more—and this was all in the same 3-month period! Then, not long after that I had to endure a messy divorce. Through all of this, I had to keep the business going and put on a smiley face for my customers and clients. Talk about stressful!

So, things don't always go to plan, and you shouldn't expect them to. You'll often be better prepared if you expect the worse.

However, there are 10 important lessons (or "golden nuggets") I've learned about running an online business around my perfect lifestyle:

Lesson #1: Incremental Action

Even if you're super busy and life tends to get in the way, it's all about taking incremental action whenever you're able.

Don't be one of those people who says, "I'll do it tomorrow when I have more time," as *life will always get in the way* and you'll *always* feel like you never have enough time.

In fact, there will be times when you struggle to spend more than 30 minutes per week working on your business. But 30 minutes per week is two hours per month, which is two hours more than you'd be able to work if you keep putting things off until the "time fairy" magically extends your day to 32 hours per day—which is never going to happen.

So, keep moving forward—even if you only have a small amount of time per week due to your busy life—and you'll continue moving in the right direction to achieve your goals.

Lesson #2: Avoid Vanity Metrics

It's not just about how much profit you make, but how much you keep. Many marketers throw sales numbers around just to inflate their own egos or to sell more of their products, but the truth is not everyone is honest about how much money they actually take home.

For example, when people create bad products intentionally just to make a quick buck, they lose a lot of it to refunds, yet they won't show those refunds in their screenshots. Also, when people are showing their Amazon earnings, they usually "forget" to mention they only take home between 1-6% of that amount in commissions.

Oh, and don't get me started on how people brag about the opt-in rate on their squeeze page being above 80%. I'd happily take a lower opt-in rate for a greater number of sales every day of the week.

Even worse is when people seek out to have a huge number of followers on social media, and some of my clients have even paid tens of thousands of dollars to do so. Yet you can't pay your mortgage with followers—you pay it with profit.

So, focus on what's important and avoid any other vanity metrics, no matter how tempting it may be.

Lesson #3: Don't Avoid Your Responsibilities

Even though it's an online business, you still have responsibilities to stay within the law and make your contributions to society.

The main thing that always screws *me* over every year is when the tax bill arrives. So, always put money aside for large unexpected tax bills from the government. We aren't immune to the normal business stuff and seeing a tax invoice for over $100,000 is scary to say the least. Having a good accountant who understands international business helps to legally reduce the amount of tax you owe though—and is so worth it.

You should also be sure to have all the correct legal documents in place (e.g. privacy policy, disclaimer, etc.), not to mention making sure all your products and sales copy is within the law. It only takes one dissatisfied customer who's had a bad day to draw attention to you, then you can lose *everything*. So, don't risk it.

Lesson #4: Your Lifestyle Should Be King

Doing things you enjoy in life is good for the soul.

If you're working all the hours in the day and feel overwhelmed with the amount of stuff you need to get done, there's nothing more productive than taking a small break. Life is here to be enjoyed!

Remember why you started this business in the first place—most likely to provide yourself with a better lifestyle. After all, it may be tempting to listen to the influencers telling you to work 27 hours per day because of the "grind," but when lying on your death bed, are you going to say, "I wish I'd have worked more."? Probably not! Instead, you'll have wished you enjoyed life more and to the fullest. Money is just a means to an end, with that end being your perfect lifestyle.

Truthfully, I could have worked my fingers to the bone to grow my business to beyond $10MM per year instead of the $750k or so per year I'm at now (as of writing this book), but I would have lost my perfect lifestyle doing so. At the relatively young age of 29 years old, I've travelled most of the world, owned a Lamborghini, bought my dream house, lived in two foreign countries, fell in love with my dream woman, experienced a lot of the incredible wonders in life and much more. Many people haven't done half of these things by the time they get to 50 years old. But most of these experiences that I'll remember forever wouldn't have been possible if I was 100% focused on my business. Personally, I'd rather *intentionally* live this better lifestyle than have more digits in my bank account that I'm too busy to use.

Not to mention that some "less than ideal" clients will have you working every hour of every day (including Sundays), regardless of whether you want to or not. So, you need to set boundaries with your time, otherwise people will walk all over you.

That's why I don't get notifications related to my business on my phone, as this ensures I don't get distracted by work when I'm trying to relax—which can often lead to anxiety. Plus, the only people who have access to my phone number are my employees. Again, it's about taking control of your time and seeing it as the most valuable thing you own.

I also work Monday to Friday, around 10am to 5pm, and sometimes a few hours on Saturday morning if I'm not busy with anything else, then have Sunday off completely.

But of course, some days I'll decide not to work *at all* if I have something exciting to do, like spending time with friends, going to special events, travelling, taking vacations, and so on. To me, that's the true definition of a business focused around your lifestyle, not the other way around.

After finishing work, I don't check my business emails or do anything that's going to generate a thought of "I'll just do this one thing quickly" while you're supposed to be relaxing. It's bad for your mental health and bad for your relationships.

This kind of lifestyle may not be possible for you when you're *just starting* your business, as you'll have to put in a lot of effort and hours to kickstart your business and begin making a profit. Not to mention that entrepreneurs are often impatient to see success. But once you've gained some traction, that's usually the best time to start designing your business around your perfect lifestyle.

After all, once you've achieved some kind of success, give yourself permission to actually *enjoy* that success!

Lesson #5: Know Your Prospects Inside Out

Research is everything.

Although it isn't sexy or exciting at first, you'll struggle to make ANY sales online without the right kind of research.

Most people skip this step because they *think* they know what their prospects want, or decide they're going to teach what they want to teach and "the right people" will find their information—but that's not how business works.

Following those kinds of ideas is only going to lead to creating something that nobody wants to buy. Even if you're a seasoned expert, it's worth double-checking what the current state of your marketplace is every now and again.

So always make sure you *truly* know your prospects inside and out.

Lesson #6: Logic vs. Emotion

Always separate your logical thoughts from your emotional thoughts.

You can't and shouldn't run a business on emotional knee-jerk reactions, otherwise you're going to make some terrible decisions.

For example, one time a customer bought my $27 product and clicked the "yes, upgrade my order" button on two of my upsells, making his order come to roughly $160. He then emailed us a few days later saying we'd "committed fraud" because we didn't have his permission to take the other two payments—keeping in mind that we *never* take payments without people's permission as that's just a real douchey thing to do.

We tried calling him to discuss this and say the payments were taken because *he* clicked the yes button, but he didn't pick up the phone. So, we replied to his support ticket explaining the above, asking him how he'd like to move forward—an instant refund, or to go through the products he'd purchased first before making a decision whether to refund or not. No reply.

The next day, we received another email from him with more accusations of how we're all "crooks" and should go to hell for being worse than the Devil incarnate. We replied to his email again, copy and pasting our original reply to him and asking him to check his emails.

Five minutes after his last email, he said he was at the police station opening an investigation and was making sure I would get "held by immigration" whenever I flew to a different country. He also threatened us with the FBI, going to the banks' headquarters in England, and so on.

At this point, my knee-jerk reaction was to turn into the Hulk, call this guy a complete ***hole and unload around three days of pent-up rage onto him. But even when the customer isn't right, you have to remain professional and reply in a logical, rational way. Despite not picking up the phone again, we tried with a different email address and magically he received our response. We let him know we'd already refunded his payments a few days ago, then after a few more emails back and forth, the whole situation was resolved.

Logically, the reason why this customer got *so* annoyed so quickly was probably because he'd been scammed before, possibly for thousands of dollars, and/or the money he had left was probably important to him for some reason. Either that, or he probably had a lot going on in his life, so he was already on a short fuse and needed to take it out on somebody else to make himself feel better and more in control.

So, before doing anything, think to yourself, *Is this an emotional decision, or a logical one?* Then rethink decisions through *logically* and approach them *rationally* and *strategically.*

Lesson #7: Copy Is King

Even if you have an amazing product, if your copy sucks, your prospects aren't going to ever see how amazing it is.

(This is typically why I think of the angle for the copy first, before I start creating the product.)

Remember, your sales pages and other marketing materials need to stir up *emotion* within your prospects and persuade them to buy of their own free will. Simply telling them about the nuts and bolts of your product and shouting at them until they buy isn't going to cut it.

That's why you should start learning how to write good copy from day one—even if you hire a copywriter—as this will increase your persuasion skills and boost your results with everything you do, including your content, your follow-up emails, your preselling pages and everything else.

Generally, the better you are at writing in a persuasive way, the easier you're going to find it to make a profit.

Lesson #8: It's Always About Your Prospects

When people first get started, they often have a few ideas for how they'd like their online business to be. Whether it's ideas for marketing angles, ideas for products, ideas for website designs, ideas for content—or pretty much anything—everything is based around their own ideas.

But there's one big problem with doing this...

You're not the one buying your products.

Or in other words, what you *think* people want probably isn't what people *actually* want.

Yep—there's a difference between the 2.

For example, in the weight loss niche, the average prospect knows they need to stop looking for the magic diet which is going to fix everything quickly (because it doesn't exist), and to change their eating and exercise habits in the long-term. So that's why most marketers will decide to create a "legitimate" weight loss program that gives people the truth. However, as soon as those same prospects find a product which promises quick results with a "new" kind of method, the prospect will often choose that over what they *should* be following.

So, as a business owner, you'll always make more money by finding out what people actually want, then give it to them—without letting your own biases and opinions influence your business.

I know this is pretty difficult to take on board as a new business owner, as it's your baby and you want to build a legacy you can be proud of. However, you can still do that—just by changing the positioning and marketing of your offers to match what people are looking for.

Now, this doesn't mean you need to sell crap. In fact, I encourage you NOT to—as you should always be trying to help people. But to sell something that people really *need*, you have to position it as something they *want*. That way, you have the best of both worlds.

You'll make a lot more sales, while people get the "aha!" moment they've been looking for.

Lesson #9: The Money Is In The List

Your email list is everything.

If the proverbial hits the fan with your traffic methods, if you have an email list, you can still generate traffic to your offers on demand, meaning even though your traffic generation stops, your income doesn't have to.

So, place a big emphasis on building that audience for the long-term!

Fortunately, this is achieved as a *side-effect* of making a profit when you use the *Profit Process* strategy explained earlier in this book.

Lesson #10: Audience Fatigue

Although your email list is important, you should never stop adding new subscribers and customers to it.

The moment you turn off the water faucet (new traffic), you're on a ticking time bomb until people stop responding to your emails. It could be six months, it could be a year, or even more—but eventually it's going to happen.

So, you should always be acquiring new customers and subscribers whether you're emailing your list regularly or not.

These are my top lessons... What about you?

What are the most important lessons **you've** learned from this experience?

Send your answers to me via our support desk at https://support.digitalprosperity.com and we may feature them in my next book :-)

WHAT NEXT?

Everything I've revealed in this book is the culmination of over 11 years of trial, error, learning, experiences and testing. These same strategies have resulted in success stories all over the world, ranging from $3,000 per month at the low end, to over $40,000 per month at the high end—and these are just the results we know about.

However, one thing we noticed with every single one of our success stories is that they started with a low-priced product (such as this book you're reading now), and soon after, joined our coaching program to get personalized help, specific to their circumstances, their business, and their ideas. After doing this, they had the focus, motivation and accountability to move forward, along with a proven plan that was specific to them that I'd personally created for them.

If you too would like to learn more about our coaching program and see if it's right for you, you can do so at www. DigitalProsperity.com/coaching/ . If you're accepted, I'll personally walk you through every step of the process to reach $10,000 in net profit per month with an online business you actually enjoy working with.

The page at the link above explains how it works and why 100% of our students (once again, as of the completion date of this book), who implemented the steps have achieved their goal of $10,000 in profit per month. And if for some weird reason it doesn't work for you, you can get *double* your money back. So, you'll make a profit either way.

If you're still unsure as to whether it'll work for you after reading the page, I'd encourage you to apply anyway, as we can discuss the finer details and answer any questions you may have during the phone conversation itself.

Otherwise, I hope you've enjoyed this book and found it valuable, and I look forward to hearing about your results!

To your success,

–James Francis.

Founder & CEO, Digital Prosperity.